SEA POWER
IN THE ATLANTIC
AND MEDITERRANEAN
IN
WORLD WAR I

Paolo E. Coletta

UNIVERSITY
PRESS OF
AMERICA

Lanham • New York • London

Copyright © 1989 by

University Press of America,® Inc.

4720 Boston Way
Lanham, MD 20706

3 Henrietta Street
London WC2E 8LU England

British Cataloging in Publication Information Available

Library of Congress Cataloging-in-Publication Data

Coletta, Paolo Enrico, 1916–
Sea power in the Atlantic and Mediterranean in World War I / Paolo E. Coletta.
p.   cm.
Bibliography: p.
Include index.
1. World War, 1914–1918—Naval operations. 2. World War, 1914–1918—Campaigns—
Atlantic Ocean. 3. World War, 1914–1918—Campaigns—Mediterranean Sea. I. Title
D580.C64   1989
940.4'5—dc19   89–5629 CIP

ISBN 0–8191–7427–0 (alk. paper)

To the memory of those who fought the war.

ACKNOWLEDGMENTS

Many persons have helped with this project. Prof. Raimondo Luraghi, University of Genova, Italy, provided the germ for the work by making it possible for me to read papers on the subject in historical conferences held in Italy in 1976 and 1978. Prof. Valeria G. Lerda, of the same University, suggested titles in Italian while her husband, Prof. Piero Lerda, who teaches French, offered French titles. Research in Italian naval sources at the Office of Italian Naval History, in Rome, was facilitated by General Gino Galuppini (GN). That office also provided the Italian translation of the official Austrian naval history of World War I and some photographs. J. David Brown, of the Naval History Library, London, made available the English translation of the official German naval history of World War I. In the United States, Dr. Richard von Doenhoff expertly provided naval sources in the National Archives; Dr. Dean C. Allard, those in the Operational Archives Branch of the Naval Historical Center; and Barbara Lynch those in the Navy Department Library. Prof. Richard A. Evans, Librarian, U.S. Naval Academy, obtained references not at hand, and Mrs. Patricia Maddox, Director of the Reference and Photographic Section of the U.S. Naval Institute, provided references and photographs.

Paolo E. Coletta

Annapolis, Md.
1 December 1988

CONTENTS

INTRODUCTION

This work is designed to be a short history of only part of the naval war fought during World War I. It touches only briefly upon the causes of the war, among which was the Anglo-German naval race beginning in 1898. It excludes naval operations in the Baltic and Black seas and the Pacific Ocean and concentrates upon the Atlantic Ocean and North, Mediterranean, and Adriatic seas, for it was in these western waters that both the Entente Powers and Central Powers believed that the war would be won or lost. Rather than in climactic battles, Jutland excepted, in those waters the naval war was fought by attrition tactics on both sides. Involved, however, were not only surface ships but aircraft and submarines, thus making the Great War the first fought in three dimensions--on the sea, over it, and under it.

Largely because of the taking of American lives by U-boats, the United States entered the war on the Allied side on 6 April 1917 but remained an Associated Power rather than ally--thus able to make her own peace terms if she wished. To some American and Allied viewers she seemed more eager to compete for supremacy in the postwar trade world and in naval power with Great Britain than to defeat the Central Powers. If the naval forces she sent across were barely enough to down the U-boat, she revealed an unsuspected capacity to build vitally needed transport and merchant shipping that made it possible to send across two million men and their supplies.

While attention is paid to the strategic and tactical decisions of naval leaders on both sides, due note is also made of the Allied coalition warfare finally made possible by the creation of the Supreme War Council and Naval Council late in 1917. However, the unwillingness of the nations involved, especially of Italy, to agree upon objectives, rendered such coalition arrangements almost futile.

With its High Seas Fleet only 60 percent as powerful as the British Home (later Grand) Fleet, Germany was unable during the first twenty-two months of the war to reduce the latter to relative equality with it by attrition tactics conducted mainly by U-boats. The first two campaigns of the latter were cut short largely because of American complaints. If German surface ships proved materially superior to British ones in the Battle of Jutland, that battle did nothing to change the strategic situation at sea. Unable to win the war on land, in 1917 and 1918 Germany resorted to all-out U-boat warfare. The United States nevertheless succeeded, with some British help, in sailing across the men and supplies that provided the winning edge for the Allied troops on the Western Front. Surprisingly, the important breakthrough for the Allies came late in 1918 on the Southeastern rather than the Western Front. In the end, Allied sea power, plus air power, plus land power--not just land power--won the war.

ILLUSTRATIONS

THE OPPOSED NATIONS AND NAVIES, AUGUST 1914

Nationalism, imperialism, and an elaborate alliance system were background causes of World War I. Nationalism included the aspiration for nationhood and additional territory by such peoples as Bulgars and Serbs. Ultranationalistic hatred and desire for revenge motivated the French, defeated by Germany in 1870-1871 and forced not only to pay a huge indemnity but to lose Alsace Lorraine. Italy sought recognition as a great power and the return from Austria-Hungary of her kinfolk (irredenti) and the territory they occupied. Imperialism, or economic and territorial expansion, became savage especially after 1879 when Germany clashed with French and British interests--and lost out on several counts. During the British war against the Boers in South Africa, Germany supported the latter. In 1904-1905 she was pro-Russian while the British were allied with the Japanese. However, the British and French were able to deny Germany a voice in the policing of Morocco in 1907 and 1911 and then froze her out of Persia. The development and support of alliances required an increase in armaments in all countries and engendered suspicions and fears among the competing nations. Britain sought to maintain a two-power standard in which her navy would be on a par with the navies of any two other navies. Particularly objectionable to her was the naval race begun by Germany in 1898 and speeded up in succeeding laws through 1912. On her part, Germany saw the Entente Powers--Britain, France, and Russia--encircle her with an iron ring.

An immediate cause of the war was the assassination 28 June 1914 at Sarajevo, Serbia, by a Serbian terrorist, of Archduke Franz Ferdinand, heir to the Austro-Hungarian throne. Expressions of sympathy rather than bellicose comments came from Europe's leaders, and little talk of war was heard for the next month. Indeed, the German Kaiser and Emperor exchanged pleasantries with a British battleship squadron invited to attend Kiel Week, the last week in June, marking the completion of the enlarged canal, and then began his usual annual cruiser to Norway. Three weeks later, however, on 23 July, Austria demanded that within forty-eight hours Serbia offer an apology, punish the guilty, cease terrorist activity and anti-Austrian propaganda, and permit Austrian representatives to serve on trials of the Serbians implicated in the assassination of Franz Ferdinand. Serbia refused the last demand, mobilized, and looked to her patron saint, Russia, for support. Austria mobilized and sought help from Germany, which promised support in a "blank check." Thereupon the German naval staff asked the Imperial Navy Office to prepare the High Sea Fleet for war. A week later that fleet concentrated in its North Sea bases while the British Grand Fleet, instead of dispersing to its various bases following exercises, also remained concentrated. Moreover, feeling that war was "by no means impossible," the First Lord of the British Admiralty, Winston Churchill, directed his ships to shadow "possible hostile men of war" and stock up on war supplies.

German attempts during the last days of July to have Austria seek mediation rather than war with Serbia fell upon deaf ears. On 28 July, when Austria declared war on Serbia, the Grand Fleet began making passage from bases along Britain's southeastern coast to Scapa Flow, in the Orkneys. On 1 August, Germany declared war on Russia--which had begun to mobilize and then lied about it--whereupon the British Foreign Minister, Sir Edward Grey, suggested mediation between Russia and Austria and also a conference at London to be attended by the Italian, French, and German ambassadors. The French rejected the first suggestion and Germany the second. Meanwhile the French concentrated their Channel Fleet at Cherbourg and Mediterranean Fleet at Toulon. When Germany declared war on Belgium on 3 August and on the fourth began to invade it, the die was cast. At 2300 on 4 August (midnight German time), Britain declared war. At 0100 on the fifth the Admiralty signalled "Commence hostilities at once against Germany."

The British well knew that the security of their islands, of their empire, even of allies, rested not only with their navy but with their merchant marine as well. ˆ In 1914, imports provided 55 percent of the protein, 61 percent of the fats, and 70 percent of the carbohydrates they consumed annually, stocks of which rarely exceeded a two months' supply. Similar figures can be given for cotton, wool, silk, jute, hemp, petroleum products, iron, rubber, aniline dyes, and optical instruments. So great was their foreign trade that in 1914 they had 43 percent of the world's shipping, the most important ships being the 3,800 steamers displacing more than 1,600 gross tons each.

To protect their shipping and to avert a collapse of credit, immediately upon the outbreak of war the British insured shippers against loss from torpedo, mine, and bomb. Moreover, their home isles served as a breakwater between Germany and the Atlantic and forced neutral or German ships making for German ports to use either the English Channel or the North Sea. Last, with command of the sea Britain and her allies could continue to trade overseas, transport troops and supplies to wherever they were needed, and conduct amphibious operations. In contrast, Germany was restricted to using land routes and denied overseas trade via the North Sea.

At the outbreak of the war, the Grand Fleet, containing 90 percent of British naval power, was based at naval stations along the southeastern coast. Supported by a predreadnought fleet in the Channel and destroyers and submarines based at Harwich, the Fleet stood ready to blockade enemy ports, defend the Western Approaches and the avenues of trade in the North Sea and English Channel, destroy overseas enemy trade, counter enemy warships that sortied from their ports, and defend the homeland from invasion. However, the new enemy, Germany rather than France or Holland, caused the Fleet to move to the northern part of the North Sea. There it would lay unprotected until new bases were provided with defenses. Further, technology posed a challenge; no navy had as yet used submarines, aircraft, or radio at war and battle ranges of 4,000 yards in 1904 had opened to 20,000. Last, since new technology made a close blockade of German ports on the North Sea impossible, the British used a distant blockade which confounded Germany because her ships, especially destroyers, were built with only small radii of action.

Rapid movement between the North Sea and the Baltic was made possible for the German High Seas

Fleet by Kiel Canal, which now could take the largest warships. Further, with complete supremacy in the Baltic, Germany could trade with Norway, Sweden, and Denmark and have her ships use the tideless sea for shakedown and other exercises. Moreover, the shallow waters of the southern part of the North Sea could easily be mined. However, because the Danes mined the Skagen and Belt, Germany must base her fleet at the mouths of the Elbe, Jade, and Weser Rivers and cover great distances to reach the Grand Fleet's northernmost bases. With no bases overseas and shortlegged ships, she could not threaten Britain's world trade, yet she was impregnable in the "wet triangle" with its apex at Heligoland and the other points at the island of Sylt and the mouths of the rivers already mentioned.

In 1914, Germany had the second largest merchant fleet in the world, to which should be added that of Austria, but from 28 July 1914 onward 623 German and 101 Austrian steamers displacing 2,875,000 tons sought refuge in neutral ports, thereby making it difficult for Germany to obtain raw materials she normally imported for manufacturing, about 30 percent of her meats and foodstuffs, and vitally needed fertilizers.

Both the Royal Navy and the German Navy followed a cautious policy. Finding it impossible to get at German ships lying in harbors behind submarines, minefields, and long-range coastal guns, the British navy dared not attack them. German leaders hoped to use the torpedoes and mines of their minor fleet to bring the Grand Fleet to approximate equality with theirs before engaging in a general battle. They also believed that the British Expeditionary Force (BEF) could much more easily be destroyed on land rather than at sea, that the war would be over before the effects of the British blockade could be felt, and that undamaged ships would serve as bargaining chips in future peace talks.

This is not to say that all British military and naval leaders agreed on war strategy. If generals wished to send a BEF to France, the First Sea Lord in 1912, Admiral Sir Arthur Wilson, opposed. Instead he would establish a close blockade of German ports, attack the Frisian Islands, and land forces on the German Baltic or Prussian coast. He had no true war plan, however, perhaps because he objected to having a naval staff, a matter corrected

4

after he was superseded by in October 1912 by Churchill. Intelligent, energetic, with military training and experience, Churchill improved war plans
and fleet organization, cooperated with the Army,
used his new submarine and air services, and brought
to the front officers who favored a distant blockade
of Germany and supported him in demanding amphibious
operations and peripheral strategy. In the matter
of material, he relieved heavily upon a former First
Sea Lord, Admiral Sir John Fisher. ⟡

In addition to her failure to meld her own naval
and military plans or to merge these with Austria's,
Germany badly erred in the assumptions upon which
she based her naval power. With her shift from Bis-
marck's "reluctant imperialism" to "world policy,"
largely due to Adm. Alfred von Tirpitz she designed a
"risk fleet" she thought would make Britain more
tractable in her international relations and capable
of defeating the British Home Fleet in a battle in
the south-central North Sea. But in seeking aggressive war against Britain Tirpitz countered his own
Foreign Office and Chancery, which sought to insure
the neutrality of Denmark, Holland, Scandinavia,
Spain, and the United States. Further, the British
responded to Tirpitz's building program in a way
opposed to that which he intended; they improved
their relations with France, Japan, and Russia, left
the French to defend the Mediterranean, and concentrated their fleet about the heart of their empire,
the waters of the English Channel and North Sea.
The British <u>Dreadnought</u>, an all-big-gun superbattle-
ship of 1905, and follow-on <u>Invincible</u>--fast,
heavily gunned, but unarmed battle cruiser--had to
be copied at great cost and a slowdown in the German
building program. In 1912, Britain had eighteen
dreadnoughts, Germany only nine. And Britain had a
long and glorious naval tradition while Germany had
none.

Tirpitz's building program also proved counter-
productive because he chose to oppose Britain's
strength in capital ships rather than exploit any
weakness he could detect in her geographical position
or navy with cruiser raiders or U-boats. He believed
that diplomacy would keep Britain quiet during the
"danger zone," the period while his fleet was being
built. In 1909 he put the end of the danger zone at
1915 and thought that his navy could defeat a British
attack by 1920, when he would have forty-one battleships, twenty battle cruisers, forty small cruisers,

and many lesser craft. Instead the British engaged in
a building race with him. Tirpitz also erred in
thinking that at war the British would institute
a close blockade of German ports and that he could
so weaken their fleet by attrition tactics that he
could then risk battle and defeat its mere remnants
in the Heligoland Bight area. Fearing the torpedo,
mine, and coastal gun, the British adopted a distant
blockade. In sum, if the High Seas Fleet fought, it
would do so at a disadvantage; if it did not, all of
Tirpitz's work would have been in vain.[4]

Moreover, while Germany could expect no help
from Austria in the North Sea, Britain could expect
help from France, the world's fourth largest naval
power, which in 1914 had a fleet built about twenty-
eight battleships--enough to check Austria in the
Mediterranean and enable British heavies based there
to return to the North Sea. Meanwhile a French
light cruiser squadron and various destroyers and
smaller craft in the Channel would cooperate with
Adm. Reginald Bacon's Dover patrol. If the French
left the North Sea largely to the British, their
Mediterranean fleet stood ready to transport home
the colonial army and agricultural supplies from
Algeria, escort convoys, and aid Italy and Britain to
guard against a possible Austrian naval menace in
the Middle Sea. As will be seen, she evacuated
thousands of Serbian troops from Albania and finally
forced Greece into the war on the Allied side.
French sailors also served as infantrymen and gunners
on the Western Front, in Greece, and at the Dardanelles.

On the other hand, grandiose French naval
building plans of 1912 never saw light. Of twelve
new battleships projected at the time, in 1914 only
two of them were operating and two were undergoing
trials. The three launched in 1913 would not enter
service until 1916. five others were never completed,
and after Italy joined the Allied side none was
needed. Her old armored cruisers were slow and her
protected cruisers and many destroyers and submarines
were so small that they could serve only for coast
defense. Further, wartime demands called for
drafting many skilled shipwrights into the army and
devoting some shipyards to the manufacture of arms
for the Western Front. In addition, by September
1914 France had lost to Germany most of its coal
supplies, iron fields, and heavy industry. The
result was that ship maintenance was delayed, little

was done to improve port facilities, and the construction of vitally needed ASW craft was delayed to
1916. In addition, the French concentrated upon
blockading the Central Powers by diplomatic and
economic rather than naval means in dealing with
Switzerland, the Netherlands, and Scandinavia. In
sum, the French naval contribution to the blockade
of Germany was mostly supportive and depended for
implementation upon British naval supremacy.

British ships outnumbered German ones but suffered various discrepancies. With mobilization
completed, Britain would have sixty-five and Germany thirty-eight battleships and other ship types in
similar proportion. The twelve British battleships
building in 1914 carried 13.5- rather than 12-inch
guns, and new construction called for 15-inch guns
and oil fired boilers that produced speed up to
twenty-five knots. The five battleships of the
Queen Elizabeth class, thus, could cross the "T" of
the High Seas Fleet no matter which way it turned.
That is, with superior speed they could cross the
head of a column of German ships and use broadside
batteries against them while only the foremost German ships could use their forward batteries. A test
mobilization of the Grand Fleet in mid July 1914
found that fleet better prepared than even Churchill
expected. On the other hand, operations would reveal
deficiencies in mines, range finders, shells, protective armor especially on battle cruisers, and
insufficient isolation of magazines from turrets.
Compared with German, British ships were inferior in
gunnery equipment, antitorpedo armament, and resistance to underwater damage. British political organization, however, was better than German. In Britain, if the First Lord and First Sea Lord disagreed,
the King could chose other men. Rather than a unified command structure, Germany divided her naval
organization into three branches--Imperial Navy
Office, Navy Office [Construction], and Admiralty
[Operations]--which failed to keep each other informed and also had made no plans for cooperating
with the army.

Only wartime operations could tell whether prewar arrangements had provided the strategic decisions, naval organization, ship numbers and characteristics, and naval leaders needed to enable the
Allies or Germany to win at sea.

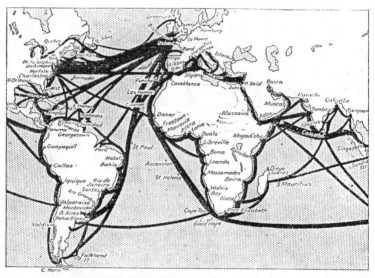

NORTH AND SOUTH ATLANTIC ROUTES

The intensity of the traffic along the main trade routes from Great Britain is depicted by the thickness of the black lines, and the map shows clearly that the North Atlantic route is the busiest in the world. Its main trade in peace time comprises passengers, high-class freight, and goods of all kinds. Other important routes are to South America and to the Cape

OPENING OPERATIONS, TO MAY 1916

With Italy declaring her neutrality upon the outbreak of the Great War, France assumed responsibility for countering the Austrian fleet and protecting British trade in the Mediterranean but left operations in the rest of the world to Britain.

Knowing that the speedy battle cruiser <u>Goeben</u> was at Pola and the light cruiser <u>Breslau</u> at Durazzo, on the Dalmatian coast, on 27 July 1914 Churchill had suggested sending a battle cruiser to the Mediterranean. He was overruled. Vice Adm. Boué Lapeyrère, commanding French naval forces in the Mediterranean, and Adm. Sir Berkeley Milne, commanding British naval forces there, had never met, corresponded, or worked out command arrangements beyond adopting a common signal code. With no ship powerful enough to counter the <u>Goeben</u>, Lapeyrère was ordered not to transport troops from Algeria to France until he had obtained command of the sea. Although Britain was not yet at war, on 30 July Churchill had directed Milne to cover Lapeyrere's transports and if possible bring the <u>Goeben</u> to action, but to avoid action against superior forces--with these undefined--except in combination with the French.

The story of the "escape" of the two German ships has been retold so many times that a barebones narration must suffice. Commanded by Rear Adm. Wilhelm Souchon, the ships sortied from the Adriatic, bombarded the embarkation points for the Algerian army as a ruse to draw Allied naval elements westward, then made for Messina, Sicily, where they coaled. Though shadowed by two British battle cruisers which easily could have sunk them, Souchon at full speed took a southeasterly course and on 10 August reached Constantinople and turned his ships over to the Turks, who on 2 August had signed a secret alliance with Germany. Questioning of Milne at the Admiralty and a court of inquiry on Milne's second in command exonerated both men and pointed instead to confusion at the Admiralty and the failure of Britain and France to have kept in close touch prior to the war. The most important results of the escape of the <u>Goeben</u> and <u>Breslau</u> were strategic rather than operational, for in late October Souchon operated against Russian forces and facilities in and along the Black Sea and thus got Turkey into the war with Russia, the ally of Britain and France.[1]

On 4 August, the day she declared war, Britain order that four to six infantry divisions and a cavalry division be sent to operate on the left flank of the French under Gen. Sir John French. Sir John suggested that troops also be sent to Antwerp but was overruled because Anglo-French naval arrangements were that no landings would be made east of Calais. Thus the road to the sea lay open for the Germans. In any event, British leaders also decided to divest Germany of her colonies, all of which threatened Allied seaborne communications and some of which, particularly in Africa, menaced British colonies.

The BEF crossed between 9 August and 8 October under naval cover and was soon joined by "Churchill's Pets," as his Royal Naval Division was known, and also by the first elements of the British naval air arm, which by the last week in September began attacking zeppelin sheds at Dusseldorf, Cologne, and elsewhere.[2] Though aware on 7 August that the BEF would cross the Channel, German generals remained unconcerned. On the eighth, four U-boats were sent to "equalize" British naval power by attacking warships escorting transports. The boats accomplished nothing, and Vice Adm. Reinhard Scheer refused to put the High Seas Fleet as a cork in the bottle at Dover Straits.[3] While German generals viewed a campaign against Britain as "a secondary matter," the British altered their traditional naval strategy by subordinating the greatest navy in the world to serve as an adjunct to the army. Except for laying some mines and sending U-boats on reconnaissance sweeps into the North Sea, the German navy remained "in-being", thus conceding command of the sea to Britain.

Intending to defeat both the BEF and the French in the strong sweep of their army's right wing through Belgium, which would then turn southwest, southeast, and so on to Switzerland, Germans saw no reason to divert troops to capture such Channel ports

ADM. BOUE LAPAYERE, COMMANDER FRENCH
NAVAL FORCES IN THE MEDITERRANEAN
    Courtesy of Paul Chack et Jean-
Jacques Antier, Histoire Maritime de
la Premier Guerre Mondiale. Paris:
Éditions France-Empire, 1970, 3 vols.
Vol. 2:240.

ADM. WILHELM SOUCHON,
GERMAN IMPERIAL NAVY

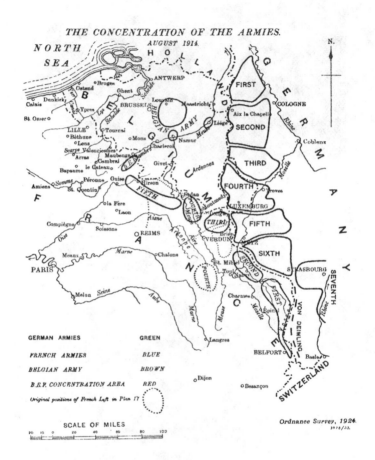

THE CONCENTRATION OF THE ARMIES.
AUGUST 1914.

GERMAN ARMIES — GREEN

FRENCH ARMIES — BLUE

BELGIAN ARMY — BROWN

B.E.F. CONCENTRATION AREA — RED

Original positions of French Left in Plan 17

SCALE OF MILES

Ordnance Survey, 1924.
3675/33.

as Dieppe, Boulogne, Calais, Dunkirk, and Ostend. Had they seized these ports, they would have controlled the Straits of Dover and caused the Grand Fleet to move south to poor harbor accommodations. Their sweep into Belgium nevertheless forced the British to shift their base from Le Havre to St. Nazaire--a move accomplished in record time and revealing the great flexibility of sea power. Moreover, although Germans seized a twenty-seven-mile stretch on the Flemish coast and built destroyer and U-boat bases there, they were stopped at the Battle of the Marne. The Western Front was destined to remain stalemated: the front lines would not move more than ten miles during the next twenty-eight months. The war would therefore be won by that coalition that lasted longer and kept up morale by assuring the provision of manpower, food, and supplies.

An early German move to "equalize" British naval power by laying mines in international waters not only provoked British retaliation but caused British naval leaders to consider mines wherever they operated.[4] A second German move was to use U-boats offensively. Both sides then resorted to sending out small forces to be ambushed and stronger forces to counterambush enemy reinforcements. On 28 August 1914 German forces fell into a trap set by the British near Heligoland and lost three light cruisers and a destroyer.[5] The Emperor thereupon directed that the High Seas Fleet be conserved for a "decisive battle," took personal control of fleet movements, and let only destroyers and submarines engage in guerrilla warfare. No major sortie occurred until November while new construction added to British strength. However, on 20 September Otto Weddigen in U-9 in one hour successively torpedoed and sank three old British cruisers patrolling off the Dutch coast in the most spectacular action in the annals of submarine warfare. Weddigen also revealed weaknesses in British ship construction, faulty dispositions, defective tactics, and poor staff work on the part of the Admiralty. While Germany augmented her U-boat campaign and built more boats, the Allies gave top priority to the development of submarine countermeasures.[6]

By this time the misnamed "race to the sea" had begun. That is, with the Western Front stalemated, both sides tried to roll the other toward the sea roughly between Antwerp and Dunkirk. Though the British shifted base back from St. Nazaire to Havre

THE EXTENSION OF THE BATTLE-LINE NORTHWARDS.
15 SEPTEMBER – 8 OCTOBER, 1914.

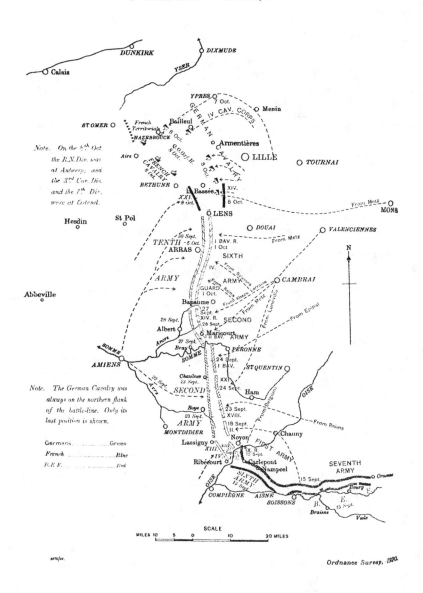

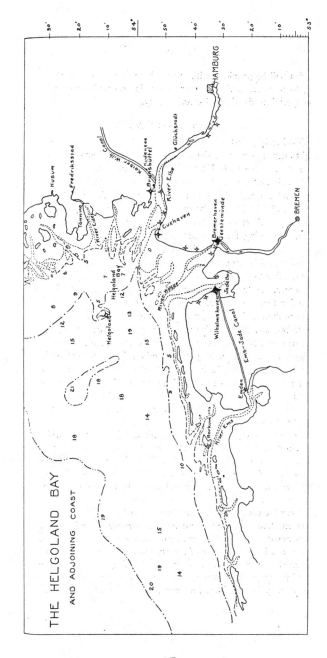

THE HELGOLAND BAY
AND ADJOINING COAST

Husum
Fredrikstad
Tönning
River Eider
Kaiser Wilh. Canal
Brunsbüttel
Audensee
Glückstadt
River Elbe
Cuxhaven
HAMBURG
Helgoland Bay
Helgoland
Bremerhaven
Geestemünde
BREMEN
River Weser
Wilhelmshaven
Jade Bay
Ems-Jade Canal
Emden
River Ems
Borkum

15

and sent troops to Dunkirk and Ostend, by 14 October Antwerp was lost. All subsequent attempts by the Dover Patrol to dislodge the Germans from the Flemish coast failed. From Ostend and particularly Zeebrugge UB and UC boats, destroyers, and minelayers operated unceasingly against the British.

On 15 October, Weddigen torpedoed and sank the British cruiser Hawke while on a sweep of the Dogger Bank. More important, on the twentieth U-17 stopped the British merchant ship Glitra off the Norwegian coast, ordered her crew into their boats, and sent a boarding party to open her sea cocks. There thus occurred for the first time in history the sinking of a merchant ship by a U-boat, a sinking that upheld the views of a minority in Germany about the value of a submarine blockade on Allied trade.

Such was the outcry about poor performance by the Royal Navy that on 28 October the First Sea Lord, the German-born but naturalized Prince Louis of Battenberg, offered his resignation. As his successor Churchill recalled the seventy-four year-old Fisher, who lacked good strategic sense but was "endowed with the cunning of the fox, the hide and memory of the elephant, and the resolution of the lion."[7] Unlike Adm. John R. Jellicoe, commander of the Grand Fleet since 3 August 1914, who told the Admiralty on 30 October that he proposed to fight only in the northern part of the North Sea, Fisher supported Churchill on the use of joint naval and military operations. Included in his greatest building program in history were 275 landing craft. Meanwhile, although Germans defeated a British squadron in the Battle of Coronel, off Chile, on 1 November, the German Far East Squadron was destroyed in the Battle of the Falkland Islands, 8 December. At about the same time five German cruiser raiders met their doom. With the outer seas "tidied up," the British ordered their overseas ships home except for some that cooperated with the French off the Dardanelles, their mission to destroy the Goeben if she sortied into the Mediterranean.

With a much better intelligence system than the Germans, the British could gain a fair idea of German naval intentions. If the shelling of the beach near Yarmouth on 2 November was designed to cover minelaying, a second attack on the coast of England in mid-November was meant to draw parts of the Grand Fleet so far south that it would enter submarine and mine areas. Backed by three battleship squadrons, Adm. Franz Hipper's cruisers bombarded Hartlepool and then Scarborough and managed to escape from the Grand Fleet and the Harwich destroyers as well with the loss of only one cruiser.[8]

On 6-7 December, a conference of the principal British and French ministers held in Paris sought to divine how to provide direct and immediate collaboration between them and their military and naval leaders in the North Sea and Mediterranean. Henceforth the French admiral commanding at Cherbourg and British admiral commanding at Dover would cooperate with land, sea, and air forces in a "Zone of the Armies of the North." Pending Gen. Joseph Joffre's plan for an offensive in the spring of 1915, a British joint operation against the Germans on the Belgian coast was postponed while others, including David Lloyd George and various British and French generals, sought a better policy than losing men in attacks on German trenches and began thinking about operations against Austria-Hungary via Salonika and to help Russia by forcing the Dardanelles. The British Admiralty considered an operation in northern Europe, against Austria in the Adriatic, an advance from Salonika in concert with Serbians and Greeks, and operations against Turkey. With neutral Holland and Denmark mitigating against moving into northern Europe, U-boats spoiling plans for attacking Austria by sea, and an attack on Turkey merely playing Germany's game, the Admiralty concluded that an attack on Ostend and Zeebrugge was the best thing to do. Just at that moment, Field Marshal Horatio Kitchener, the Secretary of War, received a cry for help against the Turks from Russia's Grand Duke, leader of both Russia's army and navy. Lacking troops, Kitchener ask the Admiralty to make a naval demonstration at the Dardanelles.[9]

On 22 January 1915 Churchill learned that Hipper intended to use cruisers and destroyers to destroy British warships in detail and annihilate the fishing fleet--presumably engaged in spying--near the Dogger Bank. Churchill directed David Beatty, commanding the battle cruisers, and Reginald Tyrwhitt, commanding the Harwich destroyer flotilla, to engage and ordered Jellicoe south from Scapa Flow. On the twenty-fourth Beatty and Tyrwhitt engaged Hipper while Scheer sortied from his bases to provide support to Hipper. The Blucher was hit and slowed,

17

and Hipper's flagship, the <u>Seydlitz</u>, was hurt, but Beatty's <u>Lion</u> was so badly damaged that he withdrew and turned command over to his second in command. Tactically, the British won the first action between squadrons of battle cruisers. The Germans lost the <u>Blucher</u> and almost a thousand of her men, and two of their ships were severely damaged, whereas the British sustained serious damage only to the <u>Lion</u>. However, the British failed to do better because of their bad system of communications and of fire control equipment and distribution and poor armor-piercing shells. Moreover, they did not learn, as the Germans did, to work additional armor onto the turrets and sides of their ships and to install flameproof scuttles between handling rooms and magazines to reduce the danger of an explosion if a flareback occurred. However, they did install fire directors and central fire control stations in their cruisers.

In material strength and compartmentation the German battle cruisers were superior to the British. Yet in the Battle of the Dogger Bank the British had won on the strategic level because Hipper had turned tail and run. Nevertheless, from the battle Hipper concluded that U-boats should be used to damage the British fleet, only homogeneous ships should be used in an operation, destroyers must be present in force, ship speed must be the greatest possible, larger magazines should be provided, and German forces must be strong enough to meet the British yet still be able to retire.[10] The Emperor, however, saw the action as conforming his earlier decision to avoid activity on the part of the High Seas Fleet, and in February he replaced its commander, Adm. Friedrich von Ingenohl, with the even more conservative Adm. Hugo von Pohl. For the next fifteen months the High Seas Fleet remained in port, meaning that action on both land and sea on the Western Front remained stalemated. By driving Germany's trade from the seas and by exercising economic pressure that strangled her, the advantage of the stalemate accrued to Britain. But how should Britain's formidable sea power be used?

Devotees of the material school argued that the Grand fleet would win the war by merely sitting. Since doing so would leave the Allied armies to fight on unassisted, Churchill countered that the Fleet should seek a climactic battle or do something that took the pressure off the Allied armies. But what strategy could be devised that would be so "insupportable . . . urgent . . . clamant, so deadly that whatever the odds [Germany's] fleet must at once be engaged?"[11] There were four possibilities: Belgium, the Baltic, the Balkans, and the Bosporus.

According to Fisher, British control of the Baltic and the landing of a Russian army near Danzig to attack either Berlin or Kiel and the Canal would force the High Seas Fleet out to sea and terrorize the German population. As alternatives he proposed landings on the Frisian coast or the coast of Schleswig-Holstein.[12] However, no agreement had been made with the Russians, the Baltic provided an awfully restricted area of operations in which U-boats could reveal their power, and the fear that damage to ships would reduce the Grand Fleet to the point that it could match the High Seas Fleet argued caution. Given their formidable defenses and the neutrality of Denmark and Sweden, seizing bases on the German, Danish, Dutch, or Scandinavian coasts also lacked appeal. There were ample old bombardment battleships and monitors to support an attack on Ostend and Zeebrugge, but both the French and Belgians opposed such an attack, the French on the ground that the British would never leave Belgium if they once took it and the Belgians because they would avoid the destruction of their towns and villages.[13] That left the Balkans and the Dardanelles.[14]

On 29 December 1914 Prime Minister Herbert H. Asquith received "two interesting memoranda," one from Churchill, one from Sir Maurice Hankey, the Royal Marine serving as secretary of the Committee for Imperial Defense (C.I.D.) Though written independently, each sought a way around the deadlock of trench warfare on the Western Front. Preferring not send new armies to "chew barbed wire in Flanders" Churchill supported Fisher's plan to seize the island of Borkum and invade Schleswig-Holstein. Hankey, however, recommended at attack on the Dardanelles, an attack Churchill had sponsored from the very beginning of the war. At a War Cabinet meeting of 8 January 1915 David Lloyd George's proposal to knock out what he called the German "props" by attacking Austria and Turkey was rejected. If General French saw no place for employing Allied troops except on the Franco-Belgian Front, most of the cabinet members eschewed Belgium, the Baltic, and the Balkans in favor of the Bosporus, especially after Churchill loosed his well-kept secret of a purely naval attack on the Dardanelles.[15] Thus began the planning of a campaign that probably has aroused more controversy than any other campaign of either World War I or World War II and about which division of opinion persists even at this writing.

Taking stock at the end of 1914, Churchill noted that the Allies had stalemated the enemy at both ends of his lines, that these ends rested on water, and that the possibility of turning a Teutonic flank lay with "the Great Amphibian." Were Turkey knocked out of the war, Russia's Western allies could provide Russia the munitions she so badly needed and Russia could not only export grains and other foodstuffs vital to the Allies but launch an offensive against Germany that would relieve the pressure on the Western Front. The venture would also greatly affect the Balkan States and perhaps bring Italy and her two million men under arms to the Allied side.[16] Asquith's daughter voiced the opinion of many that the idea of forcing the Dardanelles was "the most imaginative conception of the First World War and one which might, had all gone well, have proved the shortest cut to victory. Not only so, but in the light of what has happened since it is now recognized by many that it might have changed the course of history."[17]

Though Churchill seconded Fisher's suggestion of forcing the Dardanelles only with battleships, others at the Admiralty and Hankey as well underscored Fisher's insistence that both sides of the Straits must be secured by trained troops before transports entered the Sea of Marmora. A division would do. Kitchener, who could spare no troops, said that the operation should be tried; if it failed, the ships could be recalled. By the end of January, however, Fisher began to oppose the plan and Jellicoe to bemoan the sending of powerful ships to the Mediterranean, thereby weakening the Grand Fleet. Faced with the alternatives of concentrating on the French Front or the Eastern Mediterranean, Kitchener's own experiences led him to favor the latter. Fisher opposed, saying that he would avoid naval action against coast fortifications and mobile artillery. Further, he preferred to defeat Germany by economic pressure. In any event, on 28 January the War Council--a small group that reported to the War Committee--authorized Vice Adm. Sackville H. Carden, commanding the Aegean Squadron, to begin the operaion. Not until 26 February, however, did the War Council decide to divert the 29th Division from France to the Dardanelles, only to have Kitchener veto its use. A week later Churchill formally disclaimed any responsibility for the consequences of a military operation. Not until March, with the naval operation faltering, did Kitchener agree to send the division. Churchill's original plan for a naval demonstration had been changed to a joint operation. Enough to say that both the naval and military campaigns failed and the objective of aiding Russia went unrealized.

Both British and German commentators agree that the Allied failure at the Dardanelles lay not in the concept4ion of the plan but in its execution. The operation nevertheless caused the Balkan States to take a more favorable attitude toward the Allies and induced Italy on 4 May 1915 to denounce the Triple Alliance and sign a secret Treaty of London with the Allies who terms will be described in due course. In a great huff, however, Fisher resigned. Then a combination of factors stimulated Conservative and Unionist leaders to demand a coalition government and Churchill's head. Among these factors were the need to reorganize the Admiralty following Fisher's resignation, failure at the Dardanelles, and General French's loss of thousands of men in a vain attack on the Aubers Ridge (March), in the Second Battle of Ypres (April), in fighting at Festubert (May, and his inability to get along with Kitchener. In addition there was the growing weakness of Russia and reportedly great shortages in British shell production. While Grey and Kitchener were retained by the new government, on 17 May Churchill was notified that he must go.[16] Referring to the Dardanelles, the journalist-turned-historian Archibald Hurd wrote that there was "a deplorable miscarriage of a brilliant operation" that caused the navy to lose two men of genius, Churchill and Fisher.[19]

The War Council of the coalition government faced the same dilemmas the old government had failed to solve, yet with Churchill and Fisher gone placidity replaced pyrotechnics at the Admiralty. Rather than follow the principle of concentration advocated by the amphibious school and attack the weakest points of the Central Powers, the powers that be chose to follow the French continental doctrine of concentrating against German strength in France and Flanders, defeating it, and thus winning the war.

Although the French were weaker than the Germans, they further enfeebled themselves on their own front by giving four divisions to Gen. Maurice Sarrail for his L'Armee d'Orient at Salonika and Joffre launched a campaign in the Champagne involving forty divisions while Admiral Bacon's Dover Patrol persisted in its efforts to destroy the German works along the Flemish coast before and during the Somme campaign. With victory nowhere, the same old questions arose: should the Allies concentrate on the French Front, continue to try to force the Dardanelles, or push northward from Salonika and rescue beleaguered Serbia? In early October the British Cabinet decided to continue the attack on the Western Front, proceed with the Dardanelles, and desert Serbia. By mid october, however, the abandonment of the Dardanelles was clearly indicated. To succeed Gen. Sir Ian Hamilton there came Gen. Sir Charles Monro, a devotee of the Western Front psychology that only that strategy that killed Germans was correct and that dealing with Turks or capturing Constantinople was irrelevant. On 31 October he recommended abandonment and withdrawal, with the latter expertly accomplished with very few losses in December 1915 and January 1916. To the authors of the official British naval history the withdrawal showed "the national genius for amphibious warfare to its highest manifestation."[20] It might have been better to say that it took nine months for the British to learn enough about such operations to be able to carry one out well--and that an operation in reverse.

The consequences of failure at the Dardanelles were widespread. Serbia was destroyed; Bulgaria joined Germany; Greece and Romania remained neutral rather than joining the Allies. Turkish troops could be used against Russia, Romania, and Egypt and spawned new wars in Palestine and Syria. Twelve British and French and two Italian divisions were required to hold the Turks on the Salonika front alone. On the other hand, the defense of the Dardanelles cost Turkey dearly and the destruction of her sea power made it impossible to support her troops by sea. The burden of supplying Allied forces in the Eastern Mediterranean, added to that of countering the U-boat, greatly strained Britain's maritime resources. With hope of direct contact with Russia blasted, her fall was greatly hastened. Failure at the Dardanelles resulted in the reorganization of the Admiralty as well as of the Imperial General Staff at the War Office. The war fronts now extended not only from the Atlantic to the Alps but across the Balkans to the Near East and called for an unanticipated dispersion of Allied forces. While the Central Powers were able to defend their southern flank in the Balkans and Turkey, the Allies could mount no attack in the Baltic. All that remained at the end of 1915, evidently, was to have the Allies lose two men for one enemy in direct attacks on their barbed wire, cannon, and machine guns on the French, Flanders, and Austrian fronts in the elusive quest of the "breakthrough."

One who noisily disagreed with this procedure was Lloyd George, who sharply criticized "the billy-goat tactics of western generals in butting away the strength of their armies against unbreakable walls."[2/] The unprofitable procedure also pointed up the great need for an interallied coordinating committee that would undertake to solve the most critical Allied problem--"the achievement of effective mutual support through coordinated maritime offensives against the Central Powers."[11] Although the British and French prime ministers met in Paris on 17 November 1915 and agreed on the principle of a joint permanent committee to coordinate Allied operations, they took no steps to implement the decision. Therefore the first serious effort to obtain unity of effort was that which transpired at a conference attended by representatives of all the Allied armies held at Joffre's headquarters at Chantilly on 5-8 December. Then it was decided to delay the launching of coordinated attacks on the three major fronts--Anglo-French, Italian, and Russian--until the summer of 1916. Even though the Germans launched their great attack against Verdun on 21 March 1916, interallied cooperation was not effected. Indeed, twenty-two more months would go by before a Supreme War Council would be established, and twenty-three months, to December 1917, before an Allied Naval Council would be created.

THE FIRST BATTLE OF THE ATLANTIC, TO MAY 1916

Beginning with France in 1888, all major naval powers accepted the submarine as a fleet element, yet in 1914 even the newest boats displaced only from 500 to 800 tons. The few fitted with diesel rather than gasoline engines had not been completely tested, and some were extremely dangerous to their crews. While they might serve for defense and as fleet scouts, and perhaps attack warships, their utility against merchant ships went unrecognized. When the war began, British and French boats numbered in the sixties and seventies whereas Germany had only twenty-eight. Apparently the paucity in numbers did not bother the Germans because they believed the war would be won quickly on land and that traditional commerce raiding would not destroy enough shipping to force Britain from the war. Thus the use of the submarine as an offensive weapon came as a surprise to both sides. The British lacked enough destroyers to screen the battleships of the Grand Fleet until late 1915 and its cruisers until the end of 1916 while the Germans lacked sufficient boats to launch an effective underwater campaign until early 1915.[1]

The employment of submarines, which affected neutral as well as belligerent nations, should have followed the rules of visit and search and other matters established in international law. Were these rules followed, they would have vitiated the offensive purpose for which they were built. However, even Grand Adm. Alfred von Tirpitz saw U-boats as an equalization factor between opposing fleets rather than as commerce destroyers. While U-boats sank a British cruiser on 5 September 1914, three others on 22 September, and still another on 15 October, by this time the German flag had been driven from the outer seas. Why not, then, engage in Handelskrieg mit U-Booten--use U-boats against merchant ships.[2] On 22 October 1914, as already noted, the U-17 stopped, searched, and scuttled the little steamer Glitra off Stavanger, thus setting a model for the sinking of merchants. Then important technical improvements were made to U-boats, and their attacks revealed that the British and French knew not how to defend either merchant vessel or warship. In consequence, on 26 November all British cross-Channel sailings were stopped until they could be escorted. This done, a permanent patrol was established between British and French ends of the line and in addition decoy ships,--disguised merchant ships variously called "mystery" or "Q" ships--were sent out to seek intruding U-boats. In an interview granted on 22 December 1914 Tirpitz hinted at a future U-boat campaign against merchant ships as well as warships. That a decision had been made to attack all ships was revealed on 30 January 1915 when the U-20 fired torpedoes at merchant ships without giving warning.[3]

With their fleet designed to fight surface ships rather than U-boats, the British had to quickly adopt antisubmarine (A/S) measures. They ordered their ships to keep far part, zigzag, and vary their speed at irregular intervals. On 20 December 1914 they gathered a vast assemblage of small craft into an Auxiliary Patrol that would hunt U-boats and mines. That same month a Submarine Attack Committee established at the Admiralty began studying antisubmarine warfare (ASW) methods. In addition the British Isles were divided into twenty-three areas in which small craft hunted U-boats and minelayers. One of the most important of these areas, Dover Straits, was divided in late November 1914 into eight destroyer patrol zones. And early in January 1915 drifter nets were laid across the Straits--all without observable effect.

The last attempt to codify international law was made in the Declaration of London of 1909. In addition to establishing the rules for cruiser warfare, the declaration divided contraband into absolute and conditional classes, the remainder being free goods. However, since the declaration applied the doctrine of continuous voyage only to absolute contraband, Germany could import conditional contraband from the Baltic neutrals and from Holland as well, hence render nugatory Allied command of the sea. Moreover, free goods included metallic ores, textile materials, rubber, and other industrial products and manufactured articles which Germany could import in neutral bottoms. Gaining recognition of the doctrine of continuous voyage for such goods would therefore be a triumph for British diplomacy because it would make the ultimate destination of the goods, not the port of discharge, the test of their character.

With blockade the heart of her wartime naval strategy, Britain had declined to sign the declaration. Nor had it ever been ratified by any of the original signatories. Britain therefore devised her own maritime system for psychologically and economically strangling Germany. Royal proclamations added foodstuffs, fuels, and lubricants to the conditional contraband list and warned neutrals that these and other items were not to be reexported by them to the Central Powers. By cutting her submarine cables Britain impeded Germany's telling her story to the world while she spread Allied news that often gave a distorted picture of the war. She interfered with the sending of mail to the Central Powers and to neutrals as well. In reprisal for German minelaying and the use of the U-boat she mined international waters "in self-defense," thereby rendering such waters dangerous to neutral traffic. She armed many merchant ships and ordered them to ram U-boats if they could. By declaring the entire North Sea a military area she forced neutral ships into her hands for examination and possible detention, and on 30 January 1915 she advised her shipowners that their use of neutral flags was a legitimate ruse de guerre. She was of course delighted with the failure of legislation permitting the American government to acquire the fifty-four German and Austrian ships interned in American ports and successfully argued that her armed merchant ships in American harbors could not be interned because they were merely "defensively" armed and thus complied with international law. She embargoed various exports from her empire, as did France. In addition to applying the doctrine of continuous voyage to foodstuffs, she rationed European neutrals to the amounts of their prewar imports. In short, her control of the sea was so great that during the first eight months of the war not a single ship carrying even noncontraband reached Germany.[+]

Neutrals could either acquiesce to the British maritime system or force its abandonment by military and economic pressure. Most important was the attitude of the United States, which said it would protest each case in which its rights were violated. So pleased was Foreign Minister Grey that he proceeded to expand the contraband list with the objective

27

of securing "the maximum of blockade that could be
enforced without a rupture with the United States."
However, he would pay for damages resulting to American citizens from interference with their ships and
cargoes.[5] This decision not only hitched American
prosperity to an Allied victory but showed the United
States the advantage of having a large merchant
marine.

Direct trade between the United States and
Germany practically ceased by December 1914 while
imports from the United States that were funneled
through the Baltic countries and Holland to Germany
increased astronomically between January 1914 and
January 1915. Thereafter, however, the effects of
the Allied blockade intensified and began to suffo-
cate Germany. Her answer was to embark on 18 February 1915 upon unrestricted U-boat warfare in a
military area surrounding the British Isles.[6] Such
an undertaking was not only unacceptable in international law; it rekindled the controversy over the
treatment of commerce. Any damage Britain's maritime
system did could be settled by peaceful means; the
U-boat threatened not only neutral trade but lives as
well, a matter not subject to amicable arbitration.

Rather than complain after American life was
lost, on 10 February the United States protested the
U-boat campaign against Americans on American ships
but, to keep matters balanced, also complained
(unavailingly) to Britain about her illegal use of
neutral flag. In a note, President Woodrow Wilson
asked Germany to reconsider before destroying American property or killing American citizens. Since
such destruction of American life and property would
be an "indefensible violation of neutral rights,"
the United States would "hold the Imperial German
Government to strict accountability for such acts."[7]
On the seventeenth, Germany refused to accept responsibility for whatever happened to neutral ships
that entered her military zone.

Few U-boat attacks had been made in January and
early February, but by mid February the two U-boat
flotillas of August 1914 had grown to four, and the
year 1915 called for the construction of forty-five
new boats. U-boats sank six British or neutral ships
by the end of February and more than a score in
April. By accident or design, on 28 March U-28
torpedoed and sank the British steamer <u>Falaba</u>,
with the loss of an American passenger, and on 1 May

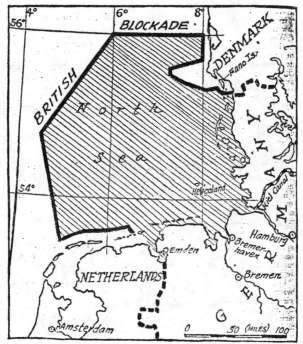

BRITISH MINED AREA

GERMAN BARRED ZONES AND BRITISH MINED AREA

a torpedo fired without warning damaged and caused loss of life on the American tanker <u>Gulflight</u> in the Irish Sea.8

Whatever good might have come from Germany's assuming responsibility and offering recompense for the attack on the <u>Gulflight</u> disappeared with the sinking of the 41,000-ton British liner <u>Lusitania</u> on 7 May off the Fastnet by a torpedo from the U-20. Of her 1,247 passengers, 785 died, among them 124 of the 159 Americans. "Seeing red" every time he thought of the <u>Lusitania</u>, Wilson could easily have led his nation to war. The time had come for the United States to decide between the U-boat and the British maritime system. On 13 May Wilson sent Germany a note in which he completely upheld the doctrine of the freedom of the seas. However, he would avoid a diplomatic rupture by giving Germany an opportunity to alter her submarine methods. Meanwhile he would hold Germany to "strict account-ability" for her every action. Although Germany refused to stop using U-boats against merchant ships, she indicated that she might do so if the United States got Britain to lift her restrictions on the rights of neutrals. While the Secretary of State, William J. Bryan, agreed, Wilson overruled him and upheld America's undoubted right to sail the seas.9 He thereby overlooked a sure way of forcing the belligerents to abide by his will--by telling either side to cease its violations of a neutral's rights on pain of his supporting the enemy.

Overlooking Germany's legalistic defense of the sinking of the <u>Lusitania</u>--she allegedly was built as an auxiliary transport and carried ammuni-tion--the State Department counselor, Robert Lansing, held that Americans on belligerent ships should be able to rely upon a U-boat's following the regular procedures for visit and search. He therefore insisted that Germany give assurance that America's rights be respected in the future. Bryan instead held that American passengers on belligerent ships were guilty of contributory negligence and that their sailing on such ships, especially if they were armed, could involve the entire nation in great difficulties. He believed that submarine warfare would cease to be a formidable threat to American neutrality if Americans could be kept off British ships and the British disarmed their merchantmen. Lansing rather than he was upheld by most members of the Cabinet, and Wilson was well on his way to deciding that the right of Americans to enjoy complete freedom to sail the seas must not be curtailed.[10]

The publication on 1 May by the German embassy in Washington of a warning that American citizens not sail on British ships traversing the German submarine war zone appeared to Lansing at least as a "formal threat" against the exercise by American citizens of "their just rights on the high seas" and an attempt by Germany to force a rupture in diplomatic relations. When Bryan charged that the cabinet was pro-Ally rather than neutral, Wilson chided him. Bryan then told Wilson privately that he must resign. On 2 June Wilson told the German ambassador in Washington, Johann von Bernstorff, that only after Germany abandoned her submarine campaign would he join her in trying to get the British to abandon their starvation policy. On 4 June, however, he reiterated the terms of his "strict accountability" note of 13 May. In a second Lusitania note he compounded national honor, international law, morality, and safety of the important trade with the Allies into an inflexible opposition on the submarine issue. Bryan thereupon resigned effective 8 June.[11] Britain need make no concessions, therefore, while Americans on board protected her passengers from U-boats.

While the Lusitania case was under discussion, Germany continued her U-boat warfare. Two new types of boats--the UB-1 and the minelaying UC-6-now operated out of Flanders. In June and July some fifty ships, thirty-one of them British, were sunk in the Southwestern Approaches alone. British minefields, cruiser squadrons, and small craft patrols notwithstanding, U-boats continued their carnage until they reached a new peak of intensity in the latter half of August, when they sank forty-two British ships displacing 135,000 tons and mines took another seven ships. In addition the U-24 torpedoed and sank the unarmed 15,000-ton White Star liner Arabic off Kinsale, Ireland. Three Americans were among her forty-four casualties. Such was the American repercussion, however, that Germany transferred most of her boats to the Mediterranean. A total of 643,000 tons of Allied shipping was lost during 1915.

Soon after receiving Wilson's second Lusitania note, Germany pledged the safety of all passenger ships. She would in addition have U-boats follow the rules of cruiser warfare against merchant ships. Last, she would give up U-boat warfare if the United States got the British to agree to abide by the Declaration of London. Fearing that the United States would break diplomatic relations, Bernstorff on his own initiative and in violation of his instructions on 2 September pledged that "Liners will not be sunk by our submarines without warning and without safety of the lives of noncombatants, provided that the liners do not try to escape or offer resistance."[12] In sum, the United States had forced Germany to abandon the unrestricted U-boat campaign she had begun in February. U-boats stopped attacking merchant ships and concentrated against British warships in the North Sea. All in all, at the cost of sixteen boats, Germany between 18 February and December 1915 sank 643,000 tons of Allied shipping including 334 British ships.

Time now for Wilson to swing the pendulum against Britain and obtain a guarantee of the freedom of the seas. Moreover, he sent his alter ego, Col. (by courtesy) Edward M. House to London, Paris, and Berlin to seek an opportunity for an American mediation effort looking toward a peace based on general disarmament and a postwar league of nations and also to press Britain hard for the relief of legitimate trade with Germany. British and French leaders would not relax their blockade policy, and in Berlin House quickly learned that Germany would not beg for peace. Rather she would seek postwar indemnities and territory in Belgium and Poland and keep open her option to resume unrestricted U-boat warfare, which she held was not illegal. If she did so, House told the French, she would drive the United States into the war. He then told the British that if Germany refused to attend the peace conference Wilson sought the United States would <u>probably</u> enter the war against Germany.[13]

At a meeting in Berlin on 30 December 1915, the Chief of the Army General Staff, Gen. Erich Falkenhayn, asserted that the military situation was so favorable that an unrestricted U-boat campaign would drive England out of the war in 1916 and that the United States would be no more dangerous as a belligerent than as a neutral. On 2 January 1916, at another meeting of military and naval chieftains, Tirpitz demanded the waging of all-out-U-boat war. Falkenhayn replied that the decision lay with the Emperor. Germany's civilian ministers, however, still opposed an unrestricted submarine war except as a last resort, with the Chancellor, Theobald Bethmann Hollweg, adding that he needed time to reach agreement with the United States on the <u>Lusitania</u> case and convince Wilson that U-boat warfare was not illegal. On 8 February, Wilson found Germany's assumption of responsibility for the death of Americans on the <u>Lusitania</u> and offer to make reparations "acceptable" if not "satisfactory." At any rate, the <u>Lusitania</u> case was settled and the threat of war disappeared. Wilson was therefore mystified when on 10 February Germany announced that on the last day of the month U-boats would sink armed merchantmen without warning.[14]

Although the U-boat had hurt British trade, at the end of a whole year it had not had a truly decisive effect on the war. Germany's naval leaders believed that a continuance of the campaign under the rules of cruiser warfare would not force Britain to seek peace. However, an unrestricted campaign would force Britain to sue for peace in six months, before the United States could render her effective aid. Unknown to the British, on 18 January the mortally ill and cautious Admiral Pohl had turned command of the High Seas Fleet over to the aggressive Reinhard Scheer, who was determined to break Britain's starvation blockade before she further augmented her strength. Too weak to oppose Jellicoe in a "decisive engagement," he would try to cut the Grand Fleet down to German size by attrition tactics. If his idea was not new, he contributed energy and intelligence to bring about the coordination of his forces and inspired his personnel with new ardor for offensive operations.

Under pressure by both naval men like Scheer and various military leaders to authorize unrestricted U-boat warfare, Pohl before his death on 23 February had agreed to take the matter under consideration. Falkenhayn added that he meant to push the Verdun salient back and detach France from Britain. Since his army could not reach Britain, he wanted U-boat attacks upon her sea lines of communication to force her to submit. Best estimates were that U-boats would sink 480,000 tons of Allied shipping a month in British waters and 125,000 tons in the Mediterranean, and that mines would account for another 27,000 tons. Multiplying 632,000 tons by six gives 3,792,000 tons, to which must be added the injurious effects of exports and imports. Were England to lose a third of her approximately 20 million tons of ships in six months she would be forced out of the war.

Chancellor Bethmann and the Emperor as well had to be convinced that the plan would not bring the United States into the war. On 18 January 1916 an American note addressed to all the Entente Powers had reiterated a demand for adherence to the rules of cruiser warfare. Though the submarine must be admitted to be a legitimate instrument for the interruption of enemy commerce, it should be brought "within the rules of International Law and the principles of humanity." Perhaps more important, a corollary declared that, because submarines were vulnerable while surfaced, merchantmen should cease to be armed. Were the proposal rejected, the United States would treat all armed merchantmen as auxiliary cruisers liable to internment. While Britain rejected the proposal, Germany read the note to mean that the United States intended to retaliate against the British blockade. Bethmann thereupon reluctantly agreed to the launching of an unrestricted U-boat campaign on condition that it be delayed until April so that he could improve diplomatic relations with the United States. German naval leaders approved the delay because it would permit the completion of some new submarines, and on 11 February they issued new orders for the conduct of unrestricted warfare: armed merchantmen and transports could be sunk but passengers ships were off limits. At the moment, the military situation for Germany was promising: she still held the territory she had conquered to the East and West; Austria was holding Italy; via Bulgaria, Germany was connected with Turkey; Britain was being repulsed in the Near East; and the U-boat was rapidly growing in power. Economically, however, Germany was suffering the effects of the blockade. Only a ruthless U-boat campaign could force Britain, and her allies as well, out of the war. Therefore the risk of war with the United States must be taken.

The new unrestricted U-boat war had just been launched when Bernstorff ran up against President Wilson, who repeated his demand that the submarine be brought "within the rules of International law and the principles of humanity," with emphasis on the latter. Nor would he let any foreign power deny Americans the freedom of the seas. Not invited to a meeting of the General Staff and the Naval High Command on 6 March, the most powerful advocate of ruthlessness in war, Tirpitz, resigned. His successor, Adm. Eduard von Capelle, supported unrestricted U-boat warfare except against passenger ships. However, an error in German thinking was exposed on 24 March when U-29 torpedoed the French cross-Channel steamer _Sussex_, with the loss of fifty of her 380 passengers but not of the five American citizens on board. The torpedoing showed bad faith and intolerable defiance to Wilson's demands for freedom of the seas. In consequence, an American note dated 18 April concluded that the United States must break diplomatic relations with her if Germany did not "immediately declare and effect an abandonment of its present methods of submarine warfare against passenger and freight-carrying vessels." According to Tirpitz, "The _Sussex_ Note was a decisive turning-point of the war, the beginning of our capitulation." He is upheld by the fact that after Scheer complied with Wilson's ultimatum and recalled his boats, some of which he detailed to operate with the High Seas Fleet, merchant ship sinkings dropped 50 percent in April alone.

On Easter Sunday and the following day, sharp debate occurred at an Imperial Council meeting. While a few would concede to Wilson on U-boat warfare as a step toward peace by his mediation, some naval officers demanded the right to wage war at least according to the rules of cruiser warfare. However, Falkenhayn would concede America nothing and concluded that the German army could not win without naval cooperation. The Emperor decided to approve the use of U-boats for military purposes but that the order to resume attacks on trade would not come, as Bethmann insisted, until "the political and military situation should demand it."[15] That moment, as will be seen, did not come until February 1917. Then, despairing of winning the war on land, Germany turned to the sea for help for its army. Meanwhile Scheer offered a suggestion that led to the only pitched naval battle of the war, off the coast of Jutland.

JUTLAND TO AMERICA'S ENTRY AT WAR

During the spring of 1916 Admirals Scheer and
Jellicoe played cat and mouse games. Denied the
unrestricted use of his U-boats, Scheer planned to
entice fractions of the Grand Fleet into traps and
then engaged it in whole or in part with his High
Seas Fleet under conditions favorable to him. On 5
March 1916 he took his fleet to the limit of the
British mine field in the Flanders Bight for a raid
on England's southeastern counties. Various elements
of the Grand Fleet tried to catch him but could not
do so.[1] During the next fortnight British cruisers
searched for German merchant vessels along the Norwegian coast while aircraft bombed aerodromes and
seaplane bases at Zeebrugge and Tondern. This time
Scheer sent his forces out too late. On 24 April he
was out again, this time to bombard towns along the
English coast. He would then decide if he should
fight or retreat if the Grand Fleet appeared. His
ships were able to shell Lowestoft for only fifteen
minutes when Reginald Tyrwhitt's Harwich forces tried
to cut him off from his bases and he retired.[2] On
3-4 May Jellicoe covered minelayers and two aircraft
carriers which sent their planes to bomb the zeppelin
sheds at Tondern. When Scheer failed to appear, he
retired.

Scheer and Jellicoe then planned almost identical operations. They would send light forces out to
be ambushed and then use heavy ships to ambush the
ambushers. Scheer would first bombard Sunderland
and mine the exits from Rosyth, where lay Admiral
Beatty and the southernmost part of the Grand Fleet.
He would send the largest concentration of U-boats
ever used in one operation to lie off Grand Fleet
bases from 17 to 13 May and have others lay mines
off these bases and defend his retreat home until 2
June. Rear Adm. Franz von Hipper, Chief of Reconnaissance, would bombard Sunderland with his battle
cruisers and light cruisers. When Beatty sortied,
whatever ships escaped the U-boats were to be led
toward the battle fleet. Because Jellicoe might

make one of his southern sweeps, Scheer would use
zeppelins for reconnaissance to the north if weather
permitted. If it did not, he would run up the
Danish coast and hit British cruisers and merchantmen
that frequented the Skagerrak. If in danger of
being overpowered, he could transit the Skagerrak and
find safety at Kiel. With bad weather making zeppelin operations impossible, he began his sortie
on the morning of 30 May. On the thirty-first he
sent Hipper to the Skagerrak as his bait.[3] Alerted
by U-boats movements and German surface ship concen-
trations, on 30 May the Admiralty directed Jellicoe
and Beatty to join eastward of the "Long Forties,"
sent three submarines to the Vyl lightship, and
directed the 3rd Battle Squadron at Sheerness and
Tyrwhitt to be ready to sail at daylight on the
thirty-first.[4]

While Jellicoe made passage for the entrance to
the Skagerrak, Beatty sailed for a point about sev-
enty miles to his southeast before joining. None
of Scheer's boats hit Beatty's ships as they sortied or was able to furnish him good information
on his intentions. Believing that Scheer was out
on just another routine sweep, Jellicoe proceeded at
only fifteen knots and wasted two hours of precious
daylight by stopping to examine neutral ships to
insure they were not Scheer's scouts.

Ordered to turn north toward Jellicoe if the
enemy did not appear by 1400, Beatty did so. Hipper
at the time was but fifty miles to the eastward.
However, his westernmost wing ship was only sixteen
miles from Beatty's easternmost wing ship. Scheer
was fifty miles astern. As Beatty turned northward,
his wing ship and Hipper's wing ship sighted each
other. Beatty thereupon raced southeastward to cut
off Hipper's retreat, not knowing that Hipper was
luring him toward Scheer. Both Beatty and Hipper
commenced firing at about the same time, but Hipper
had the advantage of seeing Beatty's ships clearly
defined against the western sky, and his gunnery was
better. Fortunately for Beatty, Rear Adm. Hugh
Evan-Thomas, with four Queen Elizabeth battleships,
came to his rescue after he lost two battle cruisers
and suffered damage to his own Lion. However, with
eight British ships against his five, at 1630 Hipper
turned eastward. At 1633, Rear Adm. William Goode-
nough, commanding the 2d Light Cruiser Squadron,
signalled both Jellicoe and Beatty that he had seen
the vanguard of Scheer's force of fifty-nine ships

38

just twelve miles ahead. Beatty thereupon turned
northwest to lure Scheer toward Jellicoe, still forty
miles away.[5]

About about 1700 Scheer turned northwestward in
an attempt to catch Beatty between him and Hipper.
Again Evan-Thomas interposed his battleships between
Beatty and Hipper and Scheer. By the end of this
action, at 1730, Jellicoe was twenty-three miles
north of Beatty, his six dreadnought squadrons in
divisions of four ships in line ahead disposed
abeam. Twenty-one miles ahead of him was Rear Adm.
Horace Hood with a battle cruiser force. Still further ahead were two more cruiser squadrons. Both
Jellicoe and Scheer proposed to fight in keeping
with their ships' characteristics. Jellicoe sought
the quick knockout blow with his heavier guns while
defending against torpedoes and mines, Scheer to
repel Jellicoe with destroyer attacks.[6]

For half an hour, while engaged with Hipper,
Beatty sent Jellicoe no intelligence. For some time
thereafter, while Beatty and Evan-Thomas tried to
bend the Germans away so that they might not see
Jellicoe, Jellicoe still received no intelligence
about the enemy.[7] He could not postpone his own
deployment much longer, but to deploy correctly he
must know exactly where the enemy was and his course
and speed. Moreover, the weather was worsening and
he and Beatty were out of position by eleven miles.
He needed four minutes to get his battleships into a
single line by simultaneous turns by division and a
full twenty minutes to get them on a fighting course.

When Jellicoe first saw Scheer, the latter was
only eleven miles away and closing at about thirty
knots. He therefore had a vital decision to make.
As Archibald Hurd put it, "In the course of minutes,
indeed seconds, Jellicoe had to decide on the manner
of the deployment of his vast armada into line of
battle. At that moment the fate of the British
Fleet, of the British Empire, of the Allied cause,
and of civilization depended on the clear tactical
vision of this one man."[8]

Jellicoe decided to deploy to port and so put
his best ships in the van. With Beatty ahead and
Evan-Thomas behind, he could cross Scheer's T and
get between him and his bases. Not until 1800,
however, was his <u>Iron Duke</u> able to fire at 14,000
yards at fleeting German shadows. Scheer was in a

predicament, for his van was enveloped by gunfire from an interminable line of huge ships along fifty degrees of an arc of circle and ships astern could bring no guns to bear. Moreover, Jellicoe's remaining on his course would cut him off from his retirement route to base. The only maneuver that would get his neck out of the noose was a simultaneous turn conducted under cover of a destroyer attack and a smoke screen. At 1833 he gave the "battle about turn" signal. As destroyers forged ahead to attack and lay smoke, all his ships turned 180 degrees in a ripple movement beginning at the rear and steered westward, toward England, while Jellicoe turned away from the attacking destroyers. Within three minutes Scheer's fleet had disappeared from Jellicoe's view, but not before four of Hipper's battle cruisers and a battleship, the last to turn, in a rift in the smoke and mist saw Hood's battle cruisers at 10,000 yards. It was the <u>Lutzow</u>'s third salvo that hit the <u>Invincible</u> between her waist turrets. She--and Hood--were destroyed when her magazines exploded. Only three officers and three enlisted men survived.[9]

Although his original deployment was as yet incomplete, Jellicoe how had to make another deployment based on a guess at Scheer's new course. He therefore kept a single line. As for his having turned away from the torpedoes launched by Scheer's destroyers, he had merely followed doctrine of which he had advised the Admiralty in October 1914. The Admiralty had approved then, and again on 5 April 1915 when he had also said that he would not be led over mines and submarines.[10] But was his doctrine appropriate for the conditions he faced? Since Scheer did not have time to prepare a mine or submarine trap, his doctrine did not apply, his critics have alleged.[11]

At any rate, given the lateness of the hour Jellicoe knew that he could not push his action to a decision and decided to keep his fleet between Scheer and his bases. When sure that he was east of Scheer, he ordered course south and reduced speed to 18 knots. Scheer, meanwhile, was steering westward. With still an hour to sunset and Jellicoe presumably interposed between him and his bases, he decided to pass astern of him in a surprise attack. At 1912 he changed course eastward. He risked another crossing of the T situation but must drive the British away from his course of retreat to Horn Reefs. Once to the east of Jellicoe, moreover, he would have his ships lighted against the western horizon. At 1908, however, while he was still highlighted by the westward light and could not see the British ships to the eastward, Jellicoe's battleships fired in a second crossing of the T situation. Again, at 1917, Scheer ordered his destroyers forward and his main body to make another countermarch battle turn. For the second time he extricated his fleet from a most perilous situation and again left Jellicoe at sea as to his whereabouts. And for the second time Jellicoe ordered the standard maneuver for avoiding torpedoes --turn away. At 1945, when Beatty informed him that Scheer was steering southwest, Jellicoe turned westward to close and destroy him. He never saw Scheer again.[12]

As one writer put it, "Twenty-eight torpedoes and a fixed determination to take no chances with his battle fleet had robbed Jellicoe of his victory."[13] But at 2110 the British saw Scheer and took him under fire. As Georg von Hase, gunnery officer of the _Derfflinger_, put it, Scheer was "In absoluten westkessel [in the frying pan.]."[14] For the third time Scheer turned away and again lost himself in the mist and darkness. He then concluded that all he could do was to steer for the Horn Reefs channel through the German mine fields. Jellicoe meanwhile decided not to engage in a night action for which his fleet was unprepared but to keep himself between Scheer and his bases and seek action at daylight, which would appear in only five hours. To insure that his own battleships would not be fired upon by them, he massed the whole of his seven destroyer flotillas to his rear and cruisers ahead, but he issued the flotillas no orders.[15]

Because Jellicoe had forged ahead with an additional knot of speed and courses converged, Scheer's screen cruisers soon came into action with Jellicoe's flotillas. Six miles ahead, Jellicoe saw firing astern but was unable to fathom its significance beyond believing that his destroyers had foiled an attack on his rear. Instead, fleet courses that had formed a V now formed an X, with Scheer cutting across his leg of it, yet he still assumed that he was between Scheer and his bases. At 2230 Scheer altered course directly for the Horn Reefs lightship. Although the Admiralty intercepted radio messages that indicated that he was heading for that point, Jellicoe rejected the information because it did not square with his own estimate of where Scheer was. While Scheer passed the Horn Reefs lightship and

41

Jellicoe turned north in preparation to engage, the Admiralty radioed him that U-boats and zeppelins were leaving Germans ports and, at 0230, that Scheer was only sixteen miles from Horn Reefs steering south at sixteen knots. He therefore knew that Scheer had returned to port.[16]

With his fleet too badly damaged to continue action, Scheer had wisely retired. Fortunately for him, the three British submarines directed to wait for him in the Amrun channel had been told to lie on the bottom until 2 June. He therefore sailed safely over them. There remained the mine field recently extended off the Vyl lightship. He was again lucky, for only the Ostfriesland hit a mine, and she was able to proceed. At 1044 Jellicoe headed for Scapa Flow.[17]

Self-effacing, cautious, and a gunnery expert, Jellicoe created trust rather than inspiration. Many writers have criticized him for lacking the aggressive spirit of Nelson, or said that "he waited on events rather than controlled them."[18] In his World Crisis, however, Churchill asserted that Jellicoe could have done better yet judged his task in light of his knowledge and point of view, the special conditions of the war, and the spirit that should inspire the Royal Navy.[19]

Jellicoe's Battle Instructions stressed defense rather than offense, specially against the torpedo, centralized control rather than independent divisional operations, reliance upon the big gun, and honored the hallowed axiom that an action must be fought with the fleet formed into a single line of ships. But was it fair to compare him with Nelson when the latter did not have to contend with torpedoes fired by surface ships and submarines and floating mines and mine fields?

Among the reasons Jellicoe did not do better were the lack of immediately relative experience by his dreadnought commanders and their lack of knowledge of history, Jellicoe's tight control over his subordinates, and failures in communications between him and his commanders and the Admiralty and him. Other reasons alleged were the neglect by British naval officers of the study of the conduct of war and a system of training and discipline that killed initiative and the taking of independent action and insisted that no move be made without direct orders from a superior.[20]

Jutland was the greatest battle fought under steam until the Battle of Leyte Gulf in October 1944. If Jellicoe had preponderant gunpower and superior speed, in torpedoes and seamanship his force about equalled that of Scheer. But with a material strength of about five to Jellicoe's eight, Scheer inflicted punishment in a ratio of eight to five even though the percentage of hits by both sides was almost equal. If British battleships were superior in design and performance to German, British battle cruisers proved vulnerable to German fire whereas German battle cruisers and light cruisers revealed great toughness and buoyancy. After the battle, however, the Grand Fleet was still twice as strong as the High Seas Fleet and Jellicoe had a reserve of five predreadnoughts in harbor, Scheer only two. Moreover, Jellicoe was ready to fight on and Scheer was not.

Strategic considerations had affected Jellicoe and Scheer in varying degree. Time was apparently on Britain's side. In control at sea, she was able to trade while denying trade to Germany. A victory by Jellicoe would have diverted energy from the navy to the army, possibly opened the Baltic to British ships which could aid the Russians, and permit attacks to be made on fortified U-boat bases. A victory by Scheer would have cut off Britain's commerce and her soldiers on the continent, kept the United States out4 of the war, and ruined the Allied cause. But Jellicoe did not total victory. As he later said, he would leave nothing "to chance in a Fleet action, because our Fleet was the one and only factor that was vital to the existence of the Empire."[21] In contrast, Scheer's defeat would not worsen the strategic situation for the High Seas Fleet. Yet Jellicoe has been criticized for being unwilling to "risk everything on one throw of the dice."[22] As Cyril Falls put it, Jellicoe "fought to make a German victory impossible rather than to make a British victory certain."[23] Jellicoe's tragedy lay in his failing to destroy an inferior fleet that had no reserves behind it. On the other hand, although the German Admiralty claimed a victory for Scheer, knowledgeable Germans concluded that the High Seas Fleet had fought very well but that the outcome at Jutland had not "affected the issue of the war."[24]

Scheer had not wrested sea power from Britain's

hand at Jutland, and because neither side won a victory the strategic situation remained unchanged. Maritime stalemate parallelled that on land, and the war was prolonged. Except for a few raids--one on 19 August 1916, one on the night of 17-18 October 1916, the last in April 1918--the High Seas Fleet failed to influence land, sea, or air operations for the rest of the war except by remaining a fleet that had to be watched. It bears repeating, however, that its mere existence prevented Britain from sending many ships to operate outside of the North Sea. Yet Jutland was the turning point of the naval war. By saving his fleet Scheer made it possible to continue German control over the Baltic, across which flowed supplies, especially of ores, that kept up Germany's fighting strength. He could also "keep the gates" about bases from which U-boats operated. Most important, he could argue that his weakened surface fleet called for the resumption of unrestricted U-boat warfare in order to destroy Britain's economic resources even if in defiance of the United States. He was eventually able to win from the new military regime installed in August 1916 with Field Marshal Paul von Hindenburg as Commander in Chief, authority to use his now seventy-four U-boats in unrestricted warfare. That warfare led to the entry of the United States into the war and Germany's defeat.

Even while operating under prize rules after the Sussex pledge of May 1916, U-boats greatly increased their toll of Allied shipping, and the appearance of the 3,000-ton submarine cruiser Deutschland exemplified the great increase in displacement, power, and range of the U-boat. Off Rhode Island, in the Mediterranean, near the Straits of Gibraltar, in the Bay of Biscay, off Ireland and Scotland, in the English Channel, North Sea, Arctic Ocean, Skagerrak, and Baltic, U-boats in the last quarter of 1916 alone sank three times more shipping than in 1915. Were this rate of sinkings to continue, it predicated the loss of two million tons in 1917, or double the total shipbuilding output of 1915 and 1916.

Scheer used his High Seas Fleet to cover the sortie and return of U-boats. In October 1916 he was authorized to resume attacks on merchant shipping but not to engage in unrestricted warfare. Alleging that the change in their employment mitigated against a large construction program, Scheer's superiors called for building only twenty U-boats per month in 1916 and only twenty-seven in 1917, and of the last only sixteen entered service. However, even when operating under prize rules the U-boat practically interned the Grand Fleet, about which Jellicoe kept two fifth of all British destroyers, and promised a complete breakdown in Allied shipping by the summer of 1917.[25] Moreover, Jellicoe and the Admiralty paid no heed to various young officers who asserted that shipping losses would be reduced by the use of convoy, by which so large a proportion of British trade had been conducted during the wars of the sailing ship era. Those opposed to convoy argued that they provided large targets, ship masters said they could not keep station, insufficient escorts were available, and convoy was wasteful because it moved at the speed of the slowest ship, jammed ports when forming up, and so dislocated distribution lines in ports of entry that they reduced cargo delivery by 30 percent.[26] Ships therefore continued to be funnelled into four patrolled routes from the Western Approaches to British and Irish ports that Lloyd George and his supporters called "death traps."[27] Yet it took its advocates until May 1917 to convince the Admiralty to adopt the convoy.

In December 1916 the great shipping losses and the ineptitude of the Allied war direction caused Britain's civil leaders to ask Jellicoe to relinquish command of the Grand Fleet and serve as the First Sea Lord and to have Lloyd George succeed Asquith as prime minister. Sir Edward Carson, the new First Lord of the Admiralty, erred in accepting advice only from the Admiralty's leaders and made no change in naval strategy. Indeed, at the end of his six-month tour he confessed that "no single magic remedy exists, or probably will exist [to counter the U-boat]." Yet he agreed that an experiment with convoy should be tried.[28]

With the war both on land and sea stalemated for twenty-nine months, Lloyd George determined that statesmen rather than military men decide strategy. Allied leaders agreed that the Western was the most important front and that the conduct of Allied military operations must be centralized. Lloyd George saw the front as stretching from Flanders to Switzerland and continuing across the Italian and Balkan fronts to the Near East. The front being one, the armies should be one also, and in each theater all Allied generals should operate under the authority of a unified commander. Correct strategy, he insisted, was to continue the strangulation blockade of Germany and attack the enemy where he was weak, not strong. Although at several interallied conferences statesmen agreed that the conduct of the war was their responsibility rather than that of generals, they failed to provide novel strategic direction. The result was that the generals continued to have their own way.[29]

Another problem was that statesmen viewed policy as including operations, matters in which they were not experts. When Lloyd George, for example, in January 1917 would help Gen. Luigi Cadorna defeat and drive Austria out of the war, after which Allied armies would press on from Italy toward Laibach and Vienna, the generals vetoed his plan.[30] The failure of Gen. Robert Nivelle's campaign on the Western Front in April so deepened Lloyd George's distrust of generals that he voiced his fear that the U-boat might drive the Allies out of the war and called for the pooling of resources and additional interallied cooperation. Before such cooperation could be achieved the Russian Revolution had begun, Czar Nicholas II had abdicated, and the crumbling of her army portended Russian's defeat. Moreover, Cadorna's attack did not start until Nivelle's campaign ended--meaning that Lloyd George had obtained very little of the interallied cooperation he sought. With disaffection in the French Army amounting in certain cases to mutiny in as many as fifty-four divisions, the idea of merely Anglo-French unity of military command fell into discard.[31]

Similarly, few Allied naval commanders old or new called for modifications in strategy except for Beatty and Capt. Murray F. Sueter, successively Captain of Airships, Superintendent of Aircraft Construction at the Admiralty, and then Director of its Air Department. Beatty asked for a staff study on how the convoy system would affect the U-boat, suggested a greatly heightened mine campaign and a tightening of the Dover Straits barrage, and thought much more use should be made of naval air power. With some misgiving, the Admiralty approved convoy on the Shetlands to Norway run. Unfortunately, Sueter's faith in the effectiveness of the naval torpedo plane was blasted when an attack on U-boats based on Cattaro, on the eastern coast of the Adriatic Sea. failed--and he never tried again.[32]

On 18 December 1916 President Wilson suggested that both the Allies and Germany state the objectives for which they fought. The Allies sought "complete restitution, full reparations, and effectual guarantees" for the future. Fearing to publicize Germany's territorial and other ambitions, Bethmann Hollweg hoped instead to get Wilson to have the Allies attend a peace conference while the forces of the Central Powers still occupied parts of Belgium, France, Italy, and Russia. Sensing a trap, the Allies rejected the overture.[33] Meanwhile, in June and again in October, Scheer renewed his demand for authority to conduct unrestricted U-boat warfare. In October, he was authorized to use U-boats only under prize rules. He realized that this procedure would enable the British to keep their fleet in northern waters while they defeated Germany by economic pressure and he had no means to cut their overseas trade lifeline. As he said, "The recognition of this necessity to attack British trade as the only means of overcoming England, made it very clear how intimate was the connection between the conduct of the war by land and by sea."[34] By the end of the year, however, the decision to resume unrestricted U-boat warfare was left to Hindenburg, thus revealing that German strategy was being determined by her military rather than civil leaders. Scheer suggested that 1 February 1917 was the latest date to start the campaign, before Britain could import the overseas harvests of 1916. America's entry into the war in consequence was deemed immaterial because she could not acquire needed tonnage in the five months the campaign would last, nor obtain crews for ships, nor send over large numbers of troops. Nor could her money make up for the shortage of supplies and tonnage. Allotting one month for the U-boats to be readied and to get into position, German leaders expected the unrestricted campaign to succeed in six months.[35]

Though statistics showed that success was mathematically certain, the German decision was a stupendous blunder. It underestimated the vigor of Allied countermeasures, called for Germany to break the British blockade and then to blockade Britain, and provoked the intervention of the United States. That intervention immediately solved the financial problems of the Allies and promised the delivery of inexhaustible material resources and manpower. In addition the entrance of the United States provided the turning point in the history of the blockade.

Heretofore, it had served as the main source of supplies that reached the Central Powers through neutrals. As a belligerent, it dried up that source.[36] However, her relatively few merchant ships and lack of a shipping organization meant that she would have to rely in part on world shipping. Last, an even more disastrous mistake was Germany's timing. Had she waited for summer to begin her unrestricted U-boat campaign, the Allies would have faced her without Russia. Without help from the United States and with Russia out of the war, France must have fallen and she could have dictated peace terms.

On 31 January Germany notified neutrals that on 1 February she would undertake "the full employment of all the weapons which are at its disposal" and establish "barred zones" about Great Britain, France, Italy, and the Eastern Mediterranean. Any ship that entered these zones would be sunk without warning. The United States, however, could send one passenger steamer each way weekly if it arrived and left on stated days from Falmouth, bore distinctive markings, followed a course dictated by Germany, and carried no contraband--a humiliating concession. On 3 February, though President Wilson severed diplomatic relations, he determined to use an armed neutrality rather than to engage in full war.[37]

Upon assuming office in March 1913, neither President Wilson nor Secretary of the Navy Josephus Daniels would increase their nation's preparedness. Both held that army and navy personnel should speak only when asked and should be denied a voice in determining national policy. Nor, despite the outbreak of the Great War, would they seek to create agencies that would enhance the coordination of foreign policy, military policy, and the logistics requirements for war. Daniels objected to the creation of a naval general staff and vetoed the preparedness recommendations offered by the purely advisory General Board of the Navy, which wanted forty-eight battleships built by 1920, and by his senior naval aide, Rear Adm. Bradley A. Fiske, Aide for Operations. Could Fiske have had his way, he would have created a naval general staff, increased naval personnel, held realistic fleet war games, have the bureaus report quarterly on their preparedness, and adopt a continuous rather than annual building program. In addition he would establish a

Council of National Defense and greatly improve naval aviation. Further, he believed that Wilson should have declared war on Germany rather than adopting neutrality, "and there would be no real risk, because the British fleet can control the seas."[36] Administration thinking, however, was that even the victor in the war would be too exhausted to challenge the United States. In his annual message of December 1914 Wilson alleged that those who demanded a preparedness program had been "thrown off balance by a war with which we have nothing to do." During that same month Daniels told the House Naval Affairs Committee that no emergency existed and countered suggestions Fiske had offered the committee for strengthening and improving the navy.[39] Moreover, rather than concentrating them in home waters, as Fiske demanded, in keeping with administration policy Daniels kept twelve battleships off Mexico's coast to protect American interests during Mexico's civil war. There they rapidly deteriorated in tropical waters and the morale of their crews sank. He also directed that while the General Board could continue to draft war plans "it must not violate neutrality by planning for war against a European belligerent."[40] However, given the great decrease in merchant ship activity by the belligerents, Wilson would build or buy merchant ships and scrap the law that prohibited the transfer of foreign ships to American registry. He also toyed with the idea of using his warships for commercial purposes and taking over the Austrian and German ships interned in American ports. On these latter points he was blocked by noninterventionists and the Allies. The result was that the British, who ruled the waves, waived the rules and controlled American trade with Europe.

So upset was Fiske with the refusal of the administration to accept his professional advice to obtain a naval general staff and build a navy strong enough to defend the nation's interests that he engaged in a mutiny with some friends in early January 1915 and wrote legislation calling for an Office of Naval Operations whose head would be "responsible for the readiness of the Navy for war and be charged with its general direction." He would also provide the Chief of Naval Operations fifteen assistants to draft war plans. Daniels was able to have the law amended so that the Chief of Naval Operations would merely be charged "with the operations of the fleet, and with the preparations and readiness of plans for its use in time of war."

He thus retained civilian supremacy but left the bureaus uncoordinated. Moreover, Fiske had to go. Rather than becoming the first Chief of Naval Operations he was rusticated at the Naval War College for the last year of his active duty. Since none of the thirteen other rear admirals, most of whom desired a naval general staff, would serve as Chief of Naval Operations, President Wilson counseled Daniels to choose a captain. Daniels selected William S. Benson, a dabbler in details lacking interest or expertise in strategy.[41] On 25 July 1915, caught between Allied and German methods for ruling the seas regardless of a neutral's rights, Wilson asked Daniels and the Secretary of War to draft "an adequate national defense program" he would present to Congress in November. Now, for the first time, he wanted professional naval advice. Evidently Fiske and other devotees of additional preparedness had made an impression after all. Later Daniels tried to take credit for creating the Office of Chief of Naval Operations, the organization that directed operations throughout the war and of course still exists.

On 15 October 1915 Wilson sent to Congress a General Board plan for a five-year building program to cost $500 million and to include 10 battleships, 6 battle cruisers, 10 cruisers, 50 destroyers, 100 submarines, and lesser craft. When Congress rejected it, he took the plan and a reiterated demand for an enlarged merchant marine to the country in a tour during January and February 1916. Yet he spoke of preparing not for war but for defense, adding that "No thoughtful man feels any panic haste in the matter." While Benson admitted the need for additional naval personnel and for officers to work on war plans, he revealed great ignorance about the capabilities of naval aviation and would build only prototype ships until Congress declared wars and provided funds for additional construction. With small-navy Democrats opposed to the continuous building program favored by Republicans, on 2 June 1916 the House voted for merely a one-year program. News then arrived of the Battle of Jutland, in which British battleships particularly had shown their worth. With Republican help, Wilson was able on 21 July to get the Senate to revive the five-year program and on 15 August got the House to approve. Among other things, the naval act Wilson signed on 29 August called for 148 combatants out of 157 ships and for starting construction on four battleships and four battle cruisers that would be the speediest and strongest in the world. These capital ships and forty-eight others must be laid down within six months, and all construction must completed in three rather than five years. Further, a Council of National Defense, a War Industries Board, and a National Research Council were created. The first would coordinate industry and war needs; the second could authorize the military services to requisition or withhold materials.[42]

In compliance with President Wilson's request of 4 February 1917 that the military departments prepare plans for full mobilization, on 24 February the General Board sent Daniels a paper entitled "Steps to be taken to meet a possible condition of war with a Central European Power." In this paper and in another dated 5 April, the board counseled the making of arrangements for the cooperation of American naval forces with those of the Allies and asked that he "immediately obtain from the Allied Powers their views as to how we can best be of assistance to them, and as far as possible conform our preparations and acts to their present needs." Among its most important recommendations the board included the sending of destroyers to cooperate with the Allies and the construction of small as well as large warships. Although Daniels and Benson declined Fiske's offer to serve on the Naval Consulting Board created on 13 July 1915 or to head the naval aviation program, they approved his working to develop a torpedo plane he had patented in 1912.[43]

President Wilson followed his policy of an armed neutrality until the "overt acts" he feared came with the sinking of eight American ships in the North Sea during the first two weeks in March. Soon thereafter the British Admiralty invited him to send an admiral to exchange views. On 28 March Rear Adm. William S. Sims, President of the Naval War College, was chosen. He had been selected despite his widely known Anglophilism, Daniels told him, adding that the President did not think the British were doing enough to prevent U-boats from reaching the Atlantic and should adopt convoying. Benson was even more a nationalist than Daniels; he was as ready to fight Britain as Germany over freedom of the sea. While he never favored intervention, he believed that the British could not win without American help, yet he would prepare for war only after Germany defeated the Allies. He therefore concentrated on building capital ships rather than AS types. Only after the war did he acknowledge that he would have augmented the preparedness of the fleet had he known that the nation would go to war, in other words that he should have been kept informed of national policy. Further, although still under civilian authority, he should have been empowered to prepare the navy as a whole, which meant authority to coordinate the bureaus. He therefore belatedly agreed with Fiske on these important points. However, Daniels refused to the eve of America's entry into the war either to admit that possibility or to ready his navy for war. He had done too little too late.

5

THE FIRST BATTLE OF THE ATLANTIC, CONCLUDED

In mid April 1917 the British and French naval commanders in Western Atlantic waters conferred with Secretary Daniels, his assistant, F.D. Roosevelt, and various American naval leaders in Washington. It was agreed that the U.S. Navy would guard the Eastern, Gulf, and Pacific coasts of the United States and the Atlantic coast of South America, thereby releasing those squadrons that had borne the duty in the Atlantic since 1914. The Americans would also take under consideration providing the British and French the destroyers they repeatedly requested.[1]

Soon after the United States entered the war British, French, Italian, Japanese, and Russian missions came to Washington to establish good will and concert financial and military matters, it being understood that the United States could extend ample credit but little immediate military or naval aid. Foreign Secretary Arthur Balfour told Daniels on 23 April that U-boats were sinking one out of every four British ships and that the Allies needed not only hundreds of destroyers, trawlers, sloops, submarines, mines, and minelayers but a token number of soldiers for France as well. With the General Board of the Navy agreeing that as many small craft as possible be sent over and that bases be provided for them, the administration decided to send up to thirty-six of its fifty-one modern destroyers over, but not until 26 July--with four precious months lost since its entrance into the war--did it change the naval building program so that precedence was given to A/S rather than to capital ships. As for aviation, an industry had to be provided for it, and it may well be that the building of merchant ships proceeded less with an eye to their wartime use than to postwar competition for world trade with Britain. At any rate, on 28 April Daniels authorized Sims to command American ships in European waters and on 24 May promoted him vice admiral.[2] Meanwhile the Export Council decided what the Allies could obtain from the United States. By controlling its exports the

53

United States also controlled Allied trade with the
neutrals, and on 9 November 1917 both the British
and French forbade experts to Holland and the
Scandinavian countries.[3]

In talks on 10 and 11 April, Admiral Jellicoe
admitted to Sims that A/S patrols against U-boats
were ineffective, voiced serious objections to
convoy, and was pleased with a new mine but could
not have enough of them manufactured to increase
their number in the Heligoland Bight and Dover
Straits let alone across the top of the North Sea.
He was happy that depth charges issued to ships had
increased from three or four in 1916 to between
thirty and forty thereafter, and he later stated that
the convoy system would have been useless against
U-boats had not escorts had many to drop on them.
But the most dismal part of his conversation was his
revelation about the U-boat situation. Asked by Sims
what he was doing about U-boats, Jellicoe replied,

> "Everything we can. We are increasing or
> anti-submarine forces in every way possible.
> We are using every possible craft we can find
> with which to fight submarines. We are building
> destroyers, trawlers, and other like craft as
> fast as we can. But the situation is very
> serious and we shall need all the assistance we
> can get."

> "It looks as though the Germans were
> winning the war," said Sims.

> "They will unless we can stop these
> losses--and stop them soon," Jellicoe replied.

> "Is there any solution for the problem?"

> "Absolutely none that we can see now."

How could the United States help? queried Sims.
Jellicoe asked for every available A/S craft with
sufficient speed to deal with U-boats and light
cruisers and submarines in addition. Sims said he
would urge his Navy Department to send as many of
these types as quickly as possible.[4]

On 14 April Sims sent to Washington the first of
a long series of cables describing the critical need
of A/S ships and merchant tonnage. He viewed American and British security interests as identical and

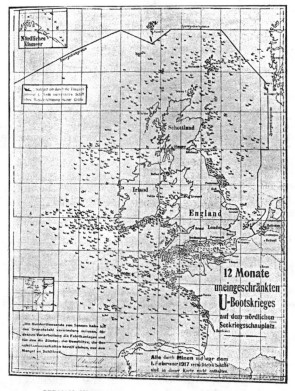

GERMAN CHART SHOWING THE SINKINGS BY U-BOATS

This was a captured chart, prepared in Germany to keep up the faith of the Germans in the success of the campaign of unrestricted U-boat warfare. Sea sinkings indicated were claimed as a result of this campaign, beginning February 1, 1917.

acknowledged British domination of the Allied naval effort. Since victory could be won only where maritime lines of communication converged in the Western Approaches, the greatest aid the United States could give Britain was to help it counter the U-boat, and he cautioned Washington that U-boat attacks along the East Coast of the United States should not divert American efforts from the Anglo-French sea front. Since building separate facilities for an American fleet would take too long and British yards were too busy to repair American ships, the United States should provide its own floating repair facilities and thus aid the Allies in a combined effort.[5]

While the American ambassador in London, Walter Hines Page, fully backed Sims, Daniels and Benson asked Sims why the British could not maintain a close blockade of the German and Belgian coasts and prevent the sortie of U-boats. Sims replied that the British were unable to do so but had the matter under continuous study. And why did the British not use convoy? Sims replied that they lacked sufficient escort ships. Again, however, the Admiralty had the subject under constant study. If the United States provided enough ships, he added, he would nudge the British to use convoy.[6] At the end of the month he wrote Mrs. Sims that "the gravity of the situation is now thoroughly understood in Washington. This means that my recommendations have been adopted practically in extenso."[7] He was wrong. The American fleet would not be fully manned until November 1917; he would not be furnished sufficient staff until early 1918; and at its peak he was given only about 21 percent of American A/S ships.

On 22 April Jellicoe sent the War Cabinet a memorandum that echoed what he had told Sims. Rather than suggesting improved methods of combating them, he concluded that the only possible counter to U-boats as the provision of additional merchant ships by the United States, which the British Shipping Controller suggested should aggregate six million tons! In consequence Sims cabled Washington about Jellicoe's ineffective A/S methods and greatly pleased Lloyd George and Sir Edward Carson, First Lord of the Admiralty, by suggesting to Jellicoe that he have studies made about convoy methods. At meetings of the War Cabinet on 23 and 25 April, Lloyd George seconded Sims on the adoption of convoy. He then told Carson he would visit the Admiralty and bring various naval officers with him. The Admiralty thereupon studied statistics provided by Comdr. Reginald Henderson of the Antisubmarine Committee and the Minister of Shipping. When he appeared, Lloyd George found the board "in a chastened mood" and willing to at least experiment with convoy. On 28 April such a convoy sailed from Gibraltar for Britain. Its safe arrival marked a turning point in the war because shipmasters had done everything they said they could not do-keep station, zigzag, and sail without lights--and proved that a convoy was no more vulnerable to a U-boat than a single ship. Most important, the convoy brought the U-boat to its escorts, so that patrol craft need not scour the ocean looking for "asparagus," as the Germans called their attack periscopes.[6]

Not until 17 May did the Admiralty establish a committee to study the convoy question. While the committee sat for three weeks, a second experimental convoy left Hampton Roads, Virginia, and arrived safely in Britain. Finally convinced, on 21 May the Admiralty adopted convoy for all incoming merchant ships, and Sims asked Daniels to adopt convoy as an offensive measure against U-boats. By early June, cruisers protected ships on the high seas and destroyers shepherded them in when they came within 300 or 400 miles of land. With Daniels approving convoying in July, regular convoys began to run from the United States, Gibraltar, and Dakar to Britain. Although Jellicoe had 279 destroyers in home waters, he allotted fewer than thirty to escort work. But the results were phenomenal. The 841,000 tons of shipping lost in April fell to 600,000 tons in May. Though losses rose to 700,000 in June, they dropped to 550,000 tons in July and then levelled off to about 350,000 tons for the rest of the war.

Because the Admiralty had been slow in adopting convoy, failed to dislodge Germans from their Flemish bases, and rejected advice from junior officers with experience at sea, Lloyd George shifted Carson to the War Cabinet and as First Lord of the Admiralty chose Sir Eric Geddes, who had already reorganized railroad transportation to and in France and currently was putting fresh life into the construction of merchant ships. Geddes agreed to take the new post on condition that Jellicoe not be removed immediately. Unable to get Jellicoe, Beatty, Reginald Tyrwhitt of the Harwich Force, and the Admiralty to pull together, he brought on board Adm. Sir Rosslyn Wester Wemyss, who was neither a Jellicoe nor Beatty man

Adm. Sir Lewis Bayly

Sir Edward Carson

and was always willing listen to ideas proposed by young officers. He also placed Rear Adm. Roger Keyes in charge of a new Plans Division in the Admiralty that would plan offensive operations in the Narrow Seas. In addition to being friendly with the King, his fluent French and passable Italian made him acceptable to these allies. Naval activity now quickened. In August, ships <u>outbound</u> from England were convoyed. Moreover, the destruction of U-boats in 1917 was three times greater than in 1916 and new construction for 1918 barely promised to replace losses.[9] Meanwhile the United States had bestirred itself and began to make its power felt in the waters of the Western Front.

Not until 4 May 1917--a month and two days after the United States entered the war--did Comdr. Joseph K. Taussig's division of six destroyers reach Queenstown, Ireland, to operate under the Commander, Western Approaches, Adm. Sir Lewis Bayly. By 1 June, however, there were twenty-four American destroyers at Queenstown, and by 1 July, twenty-eight. To these would be added the large number of small A/S craft produced by the American and British building programs for 1918.

Bayly had spent forty of his fifty years in the navy at sea. A no-nonsense man who demanded results, particularly under Sims's tutelage he was soon speaking of the American destroyers as "My destroyers" and of their personnel as "My Americans." In turn, Americans called him Uncle Lewis. As liaison with the Americans, at Sims's request, Jellicoe sent Capt. E.R.G.R. Evans, later Admiral Lord Mountevans --father of the late Lord Mountbatten--who offered advice based upon his three years' of experience in fighting U-boats with destroyers. After September, when he was transferred, Bayly often rode American destroyers. Once, when he took a week's leave, and at his suggestion, Sims assumed command in his absence, with his flag flying over the British base. Moreover, by choosing Capt. Joel R. Pringle, Sims's chief of staff at Queenstown, as his own chief of staff, Bayly insured Anglo-American cooperation.[10]

With the American ships Bayly could provide escort for shipping, for some troops transports, and also hunt U-boats. As already indicated, the number of boats destroyed in 1917 greatly increased while morale in the High Seas Fleet, which had not sortied since August 1916, fell to new lows and sparked some mutinies that were brutally punished.

Both Daniels and Benson were ignorant of conditions in Europe in part because President Wilson denied their requests to send naval observers to report at first hand. Moreover, the administration looked askance at the inability of the British "to smoke the hornets from their nests." Not until Sims reported on his talks with Jellicoe did Washington learn the gravity of U-boat campaign. In frequent letters, Sims tried to have Capt. William Veazie Pratt, Benson's assistant, and through him, Benson, see his need of staff and more ships. Though Pratt agreed with Sims's demands, Benson, and the fleet commander, Adm. Henry T. Mayo, failed to see his needs, hence did not change the 1916 construction program until July 1917 so that it favored A/S ships.[11]

Sims's relations with the British were excellent. His having been born in Canada gave him an "Imperial" connection, and for all practical purposes he was a member of the Admiralty and shared its innermost secrets. He also got along well with French naval leaders. He thus furthered maximum Allied cooperation. Yet he was in an anomalous situation. He had received no policy direction from the President and the Navy Department did not indicate his position in its organization, spell out his specific duties, supply him quickly enough with the staff, clerical aid, or the ships he needed to down the U-boat, or recognize that his office rather than the Department should coordinate matters with the Allies.[12]

Benson and Daniels saw Sims's situation differently. In fitness reports for 1915 and 1916, Benson noted that Sims was efficient when on independent duty but less so in carrying out orders from superiors. He now bristled when Sims criticized the organization and administration of his office and slowness in reaching decisions. Daniels saw Sims as merely "a transmitter of information" and assistant to Benson charged with directing the overseas war effort. Since the Department obtained information from many sources other than Sims, it could better determine worldwide wartime and postwar policy than he could from London. He was such an Anglophile that he was incapable of independent judgment. Since

British officers directed his ships' operations, he did not warrant a large staff.[13] However, relations between Sims and Benson greatly improved after Pratt by default undertook what planning was done in Operations and President Wilson on 4 July sent Sims his naval policies. The latter called for full cooperation with the Allies and aggressive action against the enemy--but the main battle fleet and coastal defense ships would remain at home.[14]

While Washington criticized the British for failing to "crush the hornets in their nests," closing the North Sea with nets and mines, and routing convoys through the U-boat danger zones, Sims said that winning the war on land required an Allied command of the sea permitted the convoy to defeat the U-boat. He did not want battleships but he should be sen4t all the A/S and merchant ships the United States built and logistic support ships as well. Further, as "the man on the spot," he should be authorized to determine operations. When Washington put pressure on him to a have the British adopt convoy and undertake offensive action against U-boat bases, he stuck to his position that his mission was "maximum cooperation with the Allies in defeating a common enemy." To carry out that mission he directly asked President Wilson for additional staff so that he could obtain a coordinated military effort. Though the Department refused to send him officers he named, all Naval War College graduates, he eventually obtained the officers he needed. However, he failed to win approval from either Wilson or Daniels for accepting an invitation to serve as an honorary member of the British Admiralty or to have Americans accept foreign decorations.[15]

By late September 1917 relations between Sims and the Department had improved. As Sims wrote Mrs. Sims, "My letters to Pratt have cleared matters up a good deal, and the officers who are frequently coming out from Washington and going back home are doing the rest." In addition, the American novelist Winston Churchill, who visited him and leading British figures as well, would stress his point of view not only in magazine articles but in talks with President Wilson. Too, Admiral Mayo, who would soon visit, should return with information "which should clear the air and which it would do if the Big Chief [President Wilson] had any confidence in the judgment of military people, which he has not."[16]

Although Wilson wished to avoid political en-
tanglements with the Allies, he wanted aggressive
action taken against U-boats and agreed with Sims's
suggestion of late July to send over a special naval
mission headed by Mayo. As Sims had predicted, Mayo
made a favorable report on his efforts after talking
with Jellicoe and British, French, Italian, and Russian representatives at an interallied naval conference held in London on 4 and 5 September. Mayo
agreed that German naval bases were impregnable but
approved the laying of a North Sea Mine Barrage
once sufficient efficient mines were available. The
conference also showed how much the Allies depended
upon the United States for aid in fighting the war
at sea, and a month after Mayo reported to it the
Department ordered mines and minelayers to lay them
in the North Sea, promised to provide cruisers for
convoy escort duty, and sent some submarines, a
monitor, and aircraft to operate from the Azores.
Thus useful steps had been taken toward fuller
interallied cooperation.[7]

     While the naval representatives met in London,
Gen. Ferdinand Foch recommended the holding of an
interallied conference in Paris to decide which
Allies would build merchant ships, provide transportation for American troops to Europe, pay for the
facilities being built in Europe for American forces,
and control neutral trade. Sims agreed that such
a conference was needed, and Lloyd George told President Wilson that the Allies had erred in concentrating on the Western Front for three years and that
the error had been made "because there has been no
body in existence. . . which could consider the military problem as a whole regardless of the tradi-
tions which have grown up in each army, and of
the national prejudices and prepossessions of the
several Allies in the use of their forces." Enemy
weaknesses, not strengths, should be exploited.
What was needed was "to create some kind of Allied
Joint Council, with permanent military and probably
naval and economic staffs attached to work out the
plans for the Allies, for submission to the several
governments concerned." Should not the purpose,
ideals, and wisdom of America be reflected in an
Allied council as well as on the field?[6] Early in
October Wilson decided that America should be
represented and appointed Col. Edward M. House to
head a mission. But he made it clear that it would
be a visiting, not a permanent, one, and that it
would be merely exploratory in nature and clear up

Josephus Daniels

Photograph by the American Press Association, New York
REAR-ADMIRAL WILLIAM S. BENSON

outstanding issues. As members he appointed Admiral Benson, Gen. Tasker H. Bliss, and representatives from the State Department, Treasury, War Trade Board, War Industries Board, Shipping board, and Food Controller. Just before the delegation sailed, Daniels gave Benson the President's instructions: "All possible cooperation but we must be free,"[19]i.e,, from political entanglement.

Lloyd George could not welcome the House mission in person because he was at Rapallo, Italy, where he was instrumental in creating a Supreme War Council that would coordinate Allied military and political actions. In the interim, Sims welcomed Benson and introduced him to Jellicoe, who told him basically what he had earlier told Mayo, adding that he favored improving naval cooperation by formalizing an Allied Naval Council. Benson agreed to the establishment of such a council and also of a planning section in Sims's office and in addition the sending of some battleships to Britain. These coal burners would replace an equal number of British ships which would be decommissioned and their crews sent to A/S work. Under Rear Adm. Hugh Rodman, battleship Division 9, eventually of five ships, operated under Beatty.[20]

Benson conducted his investigation into Sims's work without consulting him in order to form his own opinion. He reached the same conclusions Mayo had--that Sims was doing every well and that it was tim that, as Sims told Mrs. Sims, the President erase from his mind "the idea that I am hopelessly British, so much so that I can form no independent judgment." Benson then greatly pleased Sims by saying that the distrust between the Allies had lessened to the point where "they will get together in common agreement and take the necessary measures demanded by the situation."[21]

On 20 October agreement was reached on establishing a Supreme War Council, with an Allied Naval Council to follow. The British Admiralty approved the latter on 26 November, as did an interallied conference held in Paris on 29-30 November. The conference drafted a constitution for it and directed its members to prepare working papers for the first official session, which would be held on 22 January 1918. Benson won Washington's approval of the constitution and on 8 January 1918 named Sims as its

American member.

Given Benson's report, a brief review of the military situation during the second half of 1917 may prove helpful. First, by November the U-boat had been brought under control. Second, from a visit to France Benson found morale in the French army low and that "The French on the Coast could no nothing. They lacked money & everything & whatever is done there we must do."[22] Third, Gen. John J. Pershing, who arrived in France on 13 June, saw that the failure of the Allies to coordinate their actions on the French and Italian fronts helped cause the Italian defeat at Caporetto, in late October, after which both the Britain and France sent a number of divisions to help Italy.[23] This was only the third Allied operation of the war thus far that revealed cooperation--the other two being Gallipoli and the battle to clear the Flanders coast of Germans. During November, Benson had spoken with British Admiralty officials about how quickly American troops could be despatched to France and how to acquire shipping for them. On 5 December Daniels said that the United States could ship 565,000 men to France by 1 June 1918 but that he lacked half the tonnage needed to send over their supplies. On 6 December, the War Council at Washington agreed to join a committee that would ascertain if American, British, and French shipping would be available to take over the American Expeditionary Force (AEF) and its supplies. Whether American soldiers would be billetted with British and French troops or kept separated until Pershing had armies at his disposal remained moot.

Surveying the status of the war at the end of 1917, Lloyd George saw four positive improvements. With the establishment of the interallied military and naval councils, parochialism must give way to cooperation. Second, the Battle of Cambrai showed the great possibilities use of the tank had in trench warfare. Third, the U-boats was coming under control. Last, it was expected that American material and men would provide victory.[24] The material and men were slow to arrive in Europe, however.

THE AMERICAN NAVAL EFFORT

The earliest American contributions to the naval war effort included destroyers, a vanguard of aircraft pilots and mechanics, a few submarines, and some 400 submarine chasers for patrol and convoy escort duties. A second effort, that of troopships convoy, proved so successful that not a ship, soldier, or Marine out of more than two million men was lost on the passage to Europe and only three empty vessels went down on the return voyage. American ships accounted for four U-boats in 1917 and 1918, the British for the rest. Aircraft patrolling over coastal waters from American naval and air bases developed in France, England, Ireland, and Italy kept U-boats down. The American battleships sent over never fired a shell at the enemy but were available in case the High Seas Fleet somehow got by the Grand Fleet into the Atlantic. Last, the Naval Overseas Transport Service delivered several million tons of supplies.[1]

The greatly reduced effectiveness of the U-boat after April 1917 is accounted for by a number of measures. Among these were convoy itself, instruction classes for ship masters, extensive airplane and airship coverage of ships in coastal waters, the reduction of funnel smoke, and the laying of smoke-screens, which made the detection of ships difficult. There was also the augmented fitting of hydrophones, otters (mine-cutting gear depressors), paravanes (mine cutters), guns, howitzers, depth charges, and gun crews for merchant ships. In addition there were improved mines and enlarged minefields; an increase to 2,246 in the number of Allied A/S craft employed, and the growing experience of their crews, the camouflaging of ships, and unremitting work by minesweepers, "the housemaids of the ocean." An apparatus given the acronym ASDIC, after the Allied Submarine Detection Investigation Committee at Harwich, England, could obtain the range to a ship's hull several hundred yards away in 1918 by measuring underwater sound waves reflected from it.

A most singular aspect of the A/S war was the fact that with few U-boats were sunk by aircraft. Despite all the promises and high hopes of Americans involved, their naval aviation program overseas was very poor. For every six planes in the Army, the Navy had only one, and the ratio in personnel was but one to four. Airframes went to one destination, engines to another. Because American naval aviation was but six years old when the United State entered the war, there were but a dozen regular Navy pilots. Most of the airmen were in a Naval Reserve Flying Corps to which flocked largely college students, with a few coming from the naval militia Bradley A. Fiske had created in 1913. Lacking American craft, they flew British or French ones. Neither Daniels nor Benson saw value in aviation. Benson could see only two uses for aircraft--scouting and spotting shot--whereas Fiske, Sims, and various others saw dozens of uses and particularly strove to develop an effective torpedo plane, one that could launch a needed thousand-pound torpedo against a battleship. With the help among others of Naval Constructor Jerome C. Hunsaker and the Navy's Chief Constructor, Adm. David W. Taylor, the Philadelphia Naval Aircraft Factory, built in 1917, produced an F-5 that could carry such a torpedo. But the Bureau of Ordnance was not ready to conduct tests with it until 30 October 1918, Taylor was not ready until 4 November, and Benson did not approve until the fifth. It was the familiar story of too little and too late, for the Armistice was signed on the eleventh.[2]

By providing ships, submarines, and aircraft the United States was able to release the British 10th Cruiser Squadron from guarding former American trade with the neutral countries adjacent to Germany and also the 2d Squadron of the Grand Fleet and the North American and West Indies Squadrons. It also provided convoy assembly ports on its Atlantic and Gulf coasts. Further, it engaged in a tremendously large emergency merchant ship building program.

The United States made up for its lack of a transport fleet or merchant marine capable of carrying a large military expedition overseas in several ways. It undertook a huge building program, requisitioned ships on the ways, commandeered American and foreign ships in service, and seized enemy ships interned in neutral ports. Further, it obtained enemy tonnage from friendly foreign countries, purchased ships under construction in foreign yards, and contracted for new construction overseas. To administer the ship-acquisition program was the duty of the Shipping Board created by the Shipping Act President Wilson signed on 7 September 1916. Its operating organization was the Emergency Fleet Corporation, created on 16 April 1917. By August 1917 the latter had requisitioned 431 steel ships displacing more than three million tons. With the owners compensated, the board undertook to complete the ships, with 90 percent of the work accomplished by the end of 1918. To these were joined the ninety-seven German and Austrian ships displacing 700,000 tons that had been interned at the outbreak of the war. Some of these had been damaged by their crews, who thought that the holes they made in the walls of engine cylinders could not be repaired and that new ones must be cast. To the rescue came electrical welding techniques borrowed from railroad repair shops. Ironically, the former German passenger ships became the backbone of the American transatlantic ferry service, with the <u>Leviathan</u>, formerly the <u>Vaterland</u>, the largest ship in the world, taking almost 100,000 troops to France.

The Emergency Fleet Corporation supervised the building of 1,118 ships in 116 yards at a cost of more than $1 billion annually. Widely used were prefabricated parts produced by the erectors of steel buildings and steel bridges, the construction of which was suspended "for the duration." Shipping traffic itself was smoothed out by the Shipping Control Committee, which pooled all government ships. The last was able to greatly improve turnaround time in French ports and to reduce space by better packaging and stowing, and by having soldiers occupy bunks in reliefs the carrying capacity of transports was increased by 40 percent. As the number of vessels grew and turnaround time diminished, more and more men went across: 84,889 in March 18; 116,643 in April; 245,945 in May; and 278,664 in July. By 30 June a million American troops were overseas, and two million by the time of the Armistice.[3]

Stupendous growth also occurred in and under the auspices of the Bureau of Ordnance. Its personnel increased from fifty-two in early 1917 to 487 by the end of the war while its financial outlays increased from $31 million in fiscal year 1916 to $587 million in 1918. Among the major items it had produced were aerial and shipborne torpedoes, bombs, and guns; harbor defense nets; turrets, guns, mounts, and small arms for ships; ammunition, depth charges and their launching gear; fire control and optical mechanisms, the mines for the North Sea Mine Barrage; and naval railway and tractor batteries. Of particular interest were the 14-inch 50 caliber guns provided for the naval railway batteries that operated along the French front lines and during the last two months of the war fired incessantly upon railroad and supply centers and troop concentrations--with shattering effect on German morale.[4]

To transport millions of men and mountains of materials across an ocean was the task assigned the Cruiser and Transport Force created on 23 May 1917 and the Naval Overseas Transportation Service (NOTS) established on 8 January 1918. Starting with only three naval transports, Rear Adm. Albert Gleaves, commanding the transport force, gathered mail steamers, cargo carriers, and United Fruit Co. ships. To escort them he used armored, scout, and auxiliary cruisers, destroyers, converted yachts, and armed colliers. Beginning 14 June 1917, groups usually including five transports and one escort left port at two hour intervals, the fastest first in order to avoid congestion at disembarkation points. By December, all the German ships taken over had been repaired and started their runs across. With New York port crowded, Newport News, Virginia, heretofore handling cargo ships only, was used by ships that carried 40,000 troops a month to France. Altogether, eighty-eight groups left the United States for France between 14 June 1917 and 2 December 1918. Because there were not enough American ships to perform the task, beginning in May 1918 British ships were used, with 196 of them employed from first to last. After the Armistice, of course, the reverse flow began. Never had American warships experienced such continuous operations over such a long period of time as those commanded by Gleaves, nor through a winter as bad as the Atlantic had ever known. Although denied yard or drydock time, their crews, double the usual number, had kept them operating.[5]

NOTS, commanded by Comdr. Charles Belknap, grew out of several earlier formations and events dating back to March 1917 when the Wilson administration decided to arm merchant ships. To the 384 ships it armed, the Navy added all auxiliaries, formerly manned by civilian, six large oil tankers, and a number of Great Lakes ships. In December 1917 NOTS took over all War Department troopships, animal transports, and cargo transports it had chartered from the U.S. Shipping Board. In time, NOTS operated 450 ships displacing 3,200,000 tons that took across nearly six million tons of coal, fuels, food, and supplies for the military services, coal from Cardiff to Brest for the AEF, and war supplies to France and Italy. Unlike the troops transports, which carried little cargo and included British, French, and a few Italian ships, 95 percent of the cargo went over in American ships.[6]

Another great American contribution was its making possible the laying of the North Sea Mine Barrage, which Secretary Daniels called "The most daring and original naval conception of the World war."[7] Although the idea for such a barrage had come to various American as well as British leaders, the lack of mines and of defensive patrol craft precluded its establishment in 1917. Such was the vast extent of water and of its depth (from 360 to 900 feet, with an average depth of 600 feet) that many mines of an improved type would be needed. The old contact mine had short "horns" which when hit by a ship exploded its charge. To have a U-boat touch such mines meant that they must be laid close together in several layers down to about 250 feet. Fortunately, a civilian electrical engineer offered the Bureau of Ordnance a submarine gun which the bureau saw useful as mine-firing device. Both American and British mine officers then worked to adopt it to what they called the Mark VI mine. The striking advantage of this mine was its antenna, a thin copper cable kept suspended just a few feet below the surface of the water by a small metal buoy. If a hull struck the antenna, it electrically fired the 300 pounds of TNT in the mine below, with the explosion being lethal at 100 feet. Instead of 400,000 mines, now only 100,000 would be needed, which meant fewer minelayers and bases, less logistic support, and shortened laying time.[8]

Laying American mines in the North Sea Barrage was the last of a long line of events including the manufacture of the mines and of their anchors and cable mooring lines; transporting them to shipyards; building up a minelayer force; obtaining and training minelayer crews; establishing bases in Ireland and

Scotland; ,and shipping the mines over long routes party in U-boat zones. More than 500 contractors and subcontractors built mine components sufficient to produce a thousand mines a day. Involved were steel factories, foundries, machine shops, wire-rope mills, and electrical shops. Twenty-four cargo vessels took over a thousand mines on each trip to the eastern coast of Scotland, whence they were sent to new bases established at Invergordon and Inverness. The entire operation rested with Capt. Reginald R. Belknap until April 1918, when the Navy Department had him succeeded by an ordnance expert, Rear Adm. Joseph Strauss. Cooperating with Strauss was the commander of British minelayers, Rear Adm. L. Clinton-Baker, In thirteen regular and two special "excursions," ten minelayers escorted by Grand Fleet destroyers laid about 5,400 miles on each trip. Except for the premature explosion of about 4 percent of the mines, the excursions proved uneventful as the Americans laid 56,571 mines and the British 13,546 during the summer and fall of 1918.[9]

How many U-boats the barrage claimed is not known precisely. Sims said four "certainly" and six or eight "possibly," with up to eight damaged, numbers Daniels accepted.[10] Most American, British, and German writers on the subject conclude that between four and six boats were sunk and two or three damaged. But perhaps more important than the physical danger the barrage posed was its psychological effect, which helped break down German morale and by contributing to the mutiny that occurred in the High Seas Fleet in the fall of played a vital part in the overall A/S effort.

The American bridge of ships thus contributed to the Allied war effort in many ways. It provided vitally needed ships and mines for A/S warfare, battleships to backstop the Grand Fleet, and battleships and cruisers to escort the transport force. Though the United States furnished naval aircraft for ASW and bombing the enemy, its slowness in production and errors in distribution enabled it to exert little pressure in the air until very late in the war, and the dilatoriness of the Navy Department precluded the manufacture of an effective torpedo plane which Fiske, Sims, and various others believed was the only weapon that could destroy the German fleet as it lay behind otherwise impregnable defenses. Again, late in engaging the construction of merchant ships, the United States fell so badly below requirements that about half of the AEF was taken across in Allied ships. Innovative, however, were the naval railway batteries, tractor-mounted naval guns, and the antenna mine. The Navy's Cruiser and Transport Force brought two million men to France, and NOTS provided supplies. In the end, the naval support enabled American troops to provide the Allies the margin of superiority needed to defeat the Germans on land.[11]

Unable to get along with Jellicoe, and with the Admiralty under heavy fire for "slumbering" while aggressive action was needed, on 24 December 1917 Sir Eric Geddes obtained permission to dismiss him in favor of Adm. Rosslyn Wester Wemyss. On 28 December Wemyss had Rear Adm. Roger Keyes succeed Vice Adm. Reginald H. Bacon as commander of the Dover Patrol. Two U-boats had been destroyed in Dover Strait between August 1914 and 19 December 1917. Keyes had new and deep mine fields so lighted with flares and searchlights that the strait was "as bright as Piccadilly." Between January and September 1918 ten U-boats were destroyed, and large boats out of German bases stopped using the short Channel route and took the time-consuming route via the North Sea to reach the Atlantic.[12]

Wemyss and Keyes were the most important of the new British naval leaders Sims did business with and with whom, in concert with representatives from the other Allies, he tried to solve the challenging problems of coalition warfare. With respect to af-fairs at Brest, when Rear Adm. Henry B. Wilson com-manded, and at Gibraltar, where Rear Adm. Albert P. "Nibs" Niblack commanded, he was assured in January 1918 that all was going well. As Niblack put it, "If there should be a sudden lot of sinkings around Gibraltar it would raise an interesting ques-tion as to who is responsible because very morning at 10 o'clock the British, American, Italian and French representatives gather around a table and plan for the day. It is the ALLIED Conference really working with all the material available at the moment. Angels could do no more."[13] From Plymouth, too, where Rear Adm. Mark L. Bristol commanded American naval avia-tion forces, came the report that "We are working actively with the British and French. There is nothing at all that they know on this subject that has not been made available to me, and our people are in actual daily consultation with them. It is more than consultation--it is actually working with them."[14] Yet one fact that he could not hide was the inefficiency of the American naval aviation program, about which F.D. Roosevelt, in France, reported to Daniels on 19 August 1918 that "aircraft materiel arrived with missing parts & there were only 8 machines in the air."[15]

Meanwhile the detachment from the Grand Fleet of both heavy and light ships for convoy escort and A/S work provoked Beatty to suggest a change in strategy that has been ranked with Jellicoe's memorandum of 30 April 1914--in which he said he would not be led over mines and submarines--as "one of the two most important British naval documents of the war." His duty, he noted on 9 January 1918, was to defeat the High Seas Fleet in order to be able to control communications in the North Sea. However, he must subtract from his fleet those ships sent to convoy escort and other duties yet always expect that the Germans would use U-boats and lay mines along the prospective path of his fleet. He therefore concluded that "the correct strategy of the Grand Fleet is no longer to endeavour to bring the enemy to action at any cost, but rather to contain him in his bases until the general situation becomes more favourable to us." Offensive operations against the Flemish coast, minelaying off German bases, and the closing of Dover Straits would "alter the whole situation in our favour" by harassing the enemy and weakening his morale. Both the Board of Admiralty and War Cabinet agreed in principle with Beatty but noted that his policy was a temporary one that should changed once additional British and American destroyers were provided and the offensive steps he mentioned had been taken.[16]

On 20 November 1917, when Lloyd George had invited the House mission to meet with his War Cabinet and the heads of departments dealing with war activities, he said that the greatest help the United States could furnish was manpower and shipping. The naval delegate on the mission, Benson, stated that work on American capital ships had been belayed and full effort shifted to producing during the next ten months at least 267 destroyers, 103 submarines, and numerous cargo ships. As for aircraft, they would be produced by hundreds a month in January 1918 and by thousands by May or June. Benson's optimistic forecasts never materialized during the war. Moreover, while Lloyd George pointed out that 60 percent of Britain's shipping was on war service, with 2.6 million tons allotted the Allies, Bainbridge Colby, representing the U.S. Shipping Board, said that tonnage was available only to keep a 220,000 man army in France. Even merging British and American shipping would not solve the problem of sending American troops across because their transportation presented a series of difficulties--tonnage, bottlenecks in French ports and the internal French transportation system, whether the troops would be brigaded with British and French troops or kept together, and whether they would be used as substitutes for or supplements to Allied forces.[17] As noted below, these difficulties were not overcome until after the Allies counterattacked on the French Front late in July 1918.

As already noted, Lloyd George was instrumental in the creation in November and December 1917, respectively, of the Supreme War Council and Allied Naval Council. Sims was pleased with the personnel of the latter, whose first meeting was chaired by Sir Eric Geddes, with the work of the second meeting, held in Paris on 9 and 10 February 1918, and also with the third, held in Rome in mid February. As he told Mrs. Sims, the council was important because it "shifts decisions to this side--the active conduct of the war to this side," and because "The importance of [my own] position is consequently much increased. Also the importance of the command is increasing with the continuous arrival of new vessels." What a contrast to the Navy Department and Office of the Chief of Naval Operations, in which he held that "There is practically no organization--and it would be so easy to create one!" As he saw it, Captain Pratt was "carrying pretty much the whole burden" in Benson's office and "There is war to the knife between the P.D.s [Principal Dignitaries] and the C-in-C [Admiral Mayo]." The latter has demanded to be sent over here, and the matter is being considered. . . . Either the C-in-C will come here and I will quit, or he will be detached." By early March 1918, however, Sims could state that "we hear no more about the C-in-C's ambitions."[18]

Mayo was in as anomalous a position as Sims.

Although he commanded the Atlantic Fleet, Sims was in charge of the operating forces in European waters and reported to Benson rather than to him. All he could do was to have his battleships in Chesapeake Bay serve as training schools for personnel who would then be transferred to Sims or elsewhere. He wanted his fleet to go across and backstop the Grand Fleet against the German High Seas Fleet--but his battleships were not needed. Last, both President Wilson and Daniels had become convinced that Sims was doing a good job and was not the unabashed Anglophile they had formerly pictured him. He therefore would remain in London and Mayo at home.

Sims was happy not only with the Allied Naval Council but with the work accomplished by his Planning Section, much of which was accepted by the Allied admiralties, because Washington finally augmented his staff to adequate numbers, and more and more ships were joining his command. As he saw it, the problem was not in Europe but in Washington, where he thought both naval organization and administration were poor--as he would testify in a postwar investigation into the American naval war effort.[19]

Adm. William S. Sims

NAVAL WARFARE AND THE ANGLO-FRENCH FRONT, 1918

The turning point of the war both on land and sea came during the early summer of 1918. The convoy system augmented the safety of merchant shipping, the blocking by the British of the harbors of Ostend and Zeebrugge in April temporarily reduced sinkings in the English Channel to negligible numbers, and casualties from mines decreased because of the fitting of paravanes to both merchant ships and warships. Increased U-boat losses in the North Sea and Dover Straits mine barrages and elsewhere meant that the boats were now operated by inexperienced personnel who also suffered from poor morale. Allied inshore patrol boats, submarines, and aircraft made U-boat operations in inshore waters very dangerous, and by July the destruction of Allied tonnage was only 60 percent that of the first three months of the unrestricted U-boat campaign. With American and British ship construction increasing during the first half of the year, some escorts could be provided for merchant ships making for Britain and troop transports destined for French ports. Morale in the Grand Fleet remained high thanks to Beatty's imbuing his personnel with a feeling of confidence that they could give the High Seas Fleet a great drubbing if it offered battle and the moving of the fleet from austere Scapa Flow in mid April to more congenial Rosyth. Moreover, the Allied blockade, rigid bunkerage restrictions, and the limitation of American exports to Norway (April), Sweden (May), and then Holland, Denmark, and Switzerland so reduced imports by Germany from these neutrals that she had to drastically limit food and supplies for her civilian population in order to support her army. Steps were also taken to prevent Germany from obtaining the great accumulations of war materials the Allies, primarily Britain, had furnished the Russians at Archangel and Vladivostok. Further, her losses on her big push on the Western Front starting 21 March severely weakened Germany's economic stability and consequently lowered the will

of her people to continue to suffer the great priva-
tions of the two previous years. Last, with Bulgaria
out of the war, the Allies controlled the "Eastern
Corridor" and cut off supplies of oil, food, wool,
and cotton for Germany from Romania and the Ukraine.[1]

Because the British occupied all the important
northern ports and roads of France and the French
used the roads about Paris, Pershing's Americans were
assigned the southern ports of St. Nazaire, La Pal-
lice, and Bassens. Since the railroads from these
ports tended eastward, Pershing's troops could best
be used on the front between Rheims and Nancy. As
early as 10 April 1917, however, Pershing had alerted
Sims to his need of additional port and rail facilities. Sims obtained French agreement to Pershing's
use of Marseilles and several other ports and in
addition provided naval representatives to serve on
the staffs of his commanding generals in Bordeaux,
St. Nazaire, and Brest.

On 21 October 1917 Pershing's First Division
was put in a quiet sector of the French line, thus
relieving British and French troops for other duties.
Pershing's instructions were that his AEF would be
kept together and not undertake offensive operations
until it was large enough, well-enough equipped, and
sufficiently trained--which would take many months--
but President Wilson directed him to use his own
judgment on how he would use his troops following
consultations with the British and French commanders
in chief. "No other problem took up more of General
Pershing's time or attention or appeared under a
greater variety of forms," says DeWeerd, who like
Sims and many other commentators on the subject noted
that the Allies had refused to amalgamate after
three and a half years of war until adversity forced
them to do so.[2]

Because of language similarities, Sims would
have Americans join British forces. Moreover, as the
British persistently told Pershing, amalgamation
would save time, make quick use of American strength,
and release shipping for other purposes. However,
Pershing would not let Americans serve the Allies
merely as a "replacement depot" even if Britain, in
Sir Maurice Hankey's words, was "getting very near
the bottom of the man-power barrel; her resources
had to be doled out carefully to tide her over until
American reinforcements could arrive on a substantial

scale.[3] Only after the British offered to provide
shipping for them did Pershing agree to a plan in
which six full divisions would be transported in
British tonnage and therefore would not interfere
with the American shipping program.

The problems of shipping and of creating a
generalissimo and of an Inter-Allied Reserve for use
on the Western Front were turned over to an Executive
War Board of the Supreme War Council headed by Gen.
Ferdinand Foch. On 26 March, Foch was chosen to
serve in an advisory capacity as commander in chief,
but all he was authorized to do was to coordinate the
British, French, and American armies and provide them
with strategic direction for their operations along a
Western Front defined to extend "from the North Sea
to the Adriatic."[4]

In anticipation of the signing of the Treaty
of Brest-Litovsk with Russia, Gen. Erich Ludendorff
planned to launch a great offensive on the French
Front, adding to his forces there many divisions he
moved from the Eastern Front.   With the U-boat
partly conquered, he gave first priority to building
more boats and determined to gain a decision before
American troops could make their weight felt.   The
Allies held, in part because Pershing committed four
of his divisions. While the British gave priority
to shipping that would bring over six more American
divisions, Daniels and the Commandant of the Marine
Corps won approval from the War Department to send
4,500 additional Marines to France--a division had
gone over by President Wilson's order on 29 May 1917
as the advance guard of the AEF--on condition that
the Navy provide their logistic support. This Benson pledged to do. Soon Brigadier John A. Lejeune
commanded the Marine 64th Brigade, then the Fourth
Brigade, U.S. Marines, and finally, as the senior
brigadier on duty with it, the Army's Second Division, with promotion to major general.[5]

Since the beginning of the war, Allied naval
power had defended the armies' sea flank in the area
particularly between Dunkirk and Nieuport against
German invasion or bombardment. In anticipation of
the German land drive to begin on 21 March 1918,
Commo. Andreas Michelsen of the Flanders Flotilla
ordered an attack on the area on the nineteenth.
British and French ships engaged his five destroyers
and two torpedo boats and destroyed the last at the
cost of one destroyer badly damaged.   The only

attempt against the Allied-held Flanders coast had ended, to be followed in April by the last gasp of the High Seas Fleet, a raid into the North Sea that accomplished nothing.[6] Similarly, U-boats fared badly. Sinkings in March 1918 were less than half those of a year earlier, shipping replacements began to exceed losses, and by 1 May shipping sufficed for Allied needs. If the fifty-five boats operating in May sank fifty-nine British ships, sixteen boats were destroyed, making May the banner month of the A/S campaign. July produced the lowest toll of shipping since unrestricted U-oat warfare had begun in February 1917, and U-boat attacks on the East Coast of the United States and Canada failed to deter the United States from concentrating on British waters.[7]

After failing to do so in late April, in early May Keyes's Dover Patrol Flotilla blocked the harbors of Ostend and Zeebrugge in an audacious amphibious operation that remains an immortal part of the British heritage--Repington's "deathless story." It has been so well described elsewhere that retelling it here would be redundant. Even if German destroyers and U-boats based in Flanders were stopped from operating for just a few weeks, the operation had a very heartening effect upon Allied morale.[8]

Although Sims had all American naval men he could spare from other duties support the British and French armies when the Germans attacked along the Somme in April, he declined the suggestion of Pershing's Chief of the Air Staff, AEF, to place his naval air activities under one commander. He explained that naval air was an essential part of the A/S campaign, worked in conjunction with ships, and bombed enemy targets in Flanders and elsewhere. However, he promised to use his naval air to support those Allied armies within range of his bases near the coast. Lacking American-built planes, much to his chagrin his pilots flew British and French fighters and reconnaissance craft and Italian bombers.[9]

With three of Pershing's divisions engaged, the Allies checked German progress southward to the Marne at Chateau Thierry on 30 April. Also checked was a German attack in the battle of Metz in mid June. On 4 July Australian and American troops straightened out a salient line, and when Germans attacked near Rheims they were repulsed by British and American troops. On the eighteenth Foch unleased a surprise attack in which two American divisions took part and by the twenty-first had driven the Germans to defeat and retreat behind the Aisne and Vesle (Second Battle of the Marne). The Allies were thereupon able to shorten and strengthen their line in such a way that even General Ludendorff could see was the beginning of the end for Germany.

Although on 10 September the Permanent Military Representatives at the Allied Supreme War Council concluded that "the decisive defeat of the enemy coalition can only be achieved on the portion of the Western Front between the North Sea and Switzerland,"[10] the first steps leading to the debacle of the Central Powers occurred on the Southeastern Front. On 15 August Gen. Franchet d'Esperey began an attack on Bulgaria via the Vardar Valley that encouraged Austria-Hungary's subject nationalities to revolt. On the nineteenth, Gen. Sir Edmund Allenby routed the Turks at Megiddo and portended Turkey's fall. On 3 October Germany's new chancellor, Prince Maximilian von Baden, asked for an armistice and Italian troops pressed forward in Albania. On 24 October Italian troops began an advance that ended a few days later in their decisive victory at Vittorio Veneto and Austria's suing for peace. With its eastern and southern approaches soon to be in Allied hands, it would be only a question of time before Germany would be defeated. To hasten this desideratum, American naval planes that finally reached Britain and eventually Ireland and France joined the Royal Naval Air Service in covering incoming and outgoing convoys. Under Gen. Hugh Trenchard, the Inter-allied Independent Air Force formed on 6 June contained American, French, and Italian as well as British squadrons. By October, a 1,650-pound bomb was available for the Handley Page squadrons and three giant bombers were secretly being readied to attack Berlin for the first time when the Armistice intervened."

At the end of June 1918 a happy Scheer was approved by the Emperor to exercise supreme naval command subject to his orders, and Hipper was given command of the High Seas Fleet. Scheer moved his headquarters next to those of generals Hindenburg and Ludendorff, who on 12 August told him that Germany was now on the defensive and that only U-boats could win the war. But Scheer found it impossible to assume the offensive. Of the 330 new boats he ordered, only sixty-two were built, and so many boats were being sunk that new construction barely covered losses. Further, sinkings of Allied ships were so low that they could more than be made up by new construction. He also had to abandon his destroyer and U-boats bases in Flanders.[12]

Prince Max had created an awkward situation for both the Allies and President Wilson by asking for an armistice and peace negotiations based on Wilson's Fourteen Points and subsequent declarations. On 7 October, Austria's request for an immediate armistice also arrived in Washington. The French intercepted and decoded the German note, and they and the British got a jump on Wilson by asking their military and naval representatives at Versailles to draft terms. These included the liberation of all Allied countries by German troops, the immediate cessation of U-boat warfare, and the continuation of the Allied blockade. Moreover, Germany must withdraw all her surface ships and aircraft to specified bases, surrender sixty U-boats, permit the Allies to sweep mines outside of Germany's territorial waters, leave behind all naval war stores and equipment in territory Germans evacuated, and surrender Heligoland.[13] Germany replied with terms that indicated that she would evacuate occupied territory but "in such a manner that we are always ready to fight" and would cease U-boat warfare yet "its resumption must be assured."[14] To insure that the German navy would no longer operate, Wemyss wanted the naval terms of the armistice to be as consonant as possible with those of a naval peace. His suggestions, including a demand for the surrender of the High Seas Fleet, were accepted by the Allied premiers but rejected by Foch, who said that only U-boats need be surrendered, "for they alone had done any harm." Clearly, he feared that stiff terms would spur the Germans to fight on.[15]

The Allied premiers were irritated because Wilson had not consulted them and they wanted armistice terms drafted not by him but by military men. They also disagreed with his demand for the freedom of the seas, wanted concessions from Germany he had not mentioned, and would not accept terms so severe that Germany would reject them and continue fighting. For example, Beatty wanted the High Seas Fleet and Heligoland surrendered to him as commander in chief in the North Sea. Wemyss asked him to be patient and provide input into the terms to be drafted by the Admiralty for submission to the War Cabinet. The Admiralty agreed with Beatty in requiring the

surrender of the German Fleet, the only challenger
to the security of Britain's maritime communications,
opposed the freedom of the seas, and wanted terms
almost identical to those being drafted by French
naval leaders. Meanwhile, on 9 October the premiers
invited Wilson to send a representative to confer
with them. Wilson sent House.[16]

After receiving the premier's objections to
his terms, Wilson agreed to let military men write
the armistice terms and told Prince Max that he
would obtain no armistice or peace terms unless
Germany stopped her U-boat war and got rid of her
Imperial government. Max thereupon ordered U-boats
to stop sinking passenger ships and follow the rules
of cruiser warfare. However, he told Wilson that the
question of peace rested with parliament, and the
Kaiser ruefully agreed.[17] On the nineteenth Wilson
answered Austria's request for an armistice and set a
seal on the demise of the Dual Monarchy by demanding
freedom for the Czecho-Slovaks and Yugo-Slavs. Finally, on 21 October, Max told Wilson that Germany
now had a representative government and was ready
to accept armistice and peace terms.

The armistice terms drafted by Sims's planning
section and by Benson's similar organization agreed
that Germany must surrender practically uncondition-
ally so that she could not resume fighting. However,
Benson demanded the freedom of the seas and would
hold surrendered German ships in trust. House, who
reached Paris on 26 October, was notified of Benson's
ideas.[18]

While generals were quite agreed on military
terms, they disagreed on naval terms. Moreover,
naval men believed that they should write such terms.
At meetings beginning on 28 October, the Allied Naval
Council recommended to the Supreme War Council that
Germany surrender a large number of her surface ships
and U-boats while the Allies kept their blockade of
her.[19] Meanwhile Lloyd George had a brush with House
over the freedom of the seas. House said that if the
Allies did not go along with her, the United States
might have to make peace by herself and intimated
that she was rich enough to build a more powerful
navy and army than they could. Cooling down, he
then suggested that the premiers send Wilson their
objections while armistice preparations continued.[20]

On 3 November, when the premiers again objected

to House about the freedom of the seas, he compromis-
ed by postponing discussion of the matter to the
peace conference. Now the premiers were free to
discuss the armistice terms provided by the Allied
Naval Council and by Benson, and it did Sims little
good to have his planning section tell him that the
terms meant that Britain would again become the mis-
tress of the seas. By 5 November, agreement had been
reached on the final naval, military, and air terms
of the armistice. These were sent to Wilson, who
forwarded them to Germany. At 1700 on the eighth, in
a railroad car on a siding in the forest of Com-
piegne, Foch handed them to a German delegation
and gave them seventy-two hours to accept them. At
0510 on 11 November, the German Secretary of State
signed them and at 1100 the firing ceased.[21]

At an emergency meeting of the Allied Naval
Council, Wemyss obtained agreement that the High
Seas Fleet would surrender at Scapa Flow and that
Beatty would enforce the naval clause relating to its
internment. With plans ready, the Allies threw their
warmaking machinery into reverse, with Benson and
Sims agreed that the American navy should "get
clear" of Europe as soon as possible.[22]

On 15 November, as arranged between Beatty and
Hipper, Rear Adm. Hugo Meurer called on Beatty. At
Scapa Flow on 21 November, with Sims present, Beatty
formed the Grand Fleet and some American and French
ships into two parallel lines between which the
ships of the High Seas Fleet, disarmed and with
skeleton crews, sailed and then anchored. Among them
were some veteran battleships and battle cruisers
Beatty had fought at Jutland. As Beatty told a
friend, "I am now in the position of commanding the
High Sea Fleet as well as the Grand Fleet."[23] Approximately 176 U-boats, meanwhile, proceeded at various
times to Harwich to surrender to Tyrwhitt.

Although German Socialists and Communists have
tried to take credit for persuading the enlisted
corps to revolt and join the proletariat, there were
more important reasons for the mutiny that occurred
in the German Navy beginning in late October. Among
them were inadequate rations, abysmal living conditions, special treatment for officers and harsh
treatment by them, great inactivity, war weariness, a
desire to end the slaughter of war, and very low
morale.

Scheer was extremely jealous of the honor and prestige of his navy and its officers. Once granted supreme naval power, he may have dreamed of a <u>Flot-tenvorstoss</u> (death ride) that would enable his fleet to gain glory before the war ended. In this he was abetted by his own chief of staff and the chief of staff of Admiral Hipper, both of whom opposed democracy and the idea of a negotiated peace. Although he submitted when President Wilson demanded the cessation of U-boats attacks on passenger ships, he would use U-boats for an operation he had planned in contravention of his government's orders--and which his ships' crews knew about long before he issued his operation order. He would send his U-boats to sever British communications with France. When the Grand Fleet steamed south from Rosyth, it would be attacked with torpedoes and mines. After it had suffered attrition, he would engage it with the High Seas Fleet.[24] But when he ordered his ships to assemble at Wilhelmshaven on the twenty-ninth, the men refused to sail their ships. When branded as traitors and threatened with sharp reprisals, on the thirtieth they engaged in a full-fledged rebellion that overthrew the officer corps, sent the Imperial Navy into its death throes, and soon spread from naval ports to other centers. In his memoirs,Scheer sought to shift the blame for the rebellion and the collapse of his navy from the incompetence of his officers to a treasonable socialist or communist conspiracy that simply did not exist.[25]

NAVAL WARFARE IN THE MEDITERRANEAN
AND ADRIATIC, 1918

From 1882 to 1914, Italy was allied with Germany and Austria against France. However, Italy desired to improve the unfavorable frontier established at the end of the Austro-Italian war of 1866 and asked Austria what compensation she would offer as recompense for her having annexed Bosnia and Herzegovina in 1908. When Austria's reply proved unsatisfactory, Italy turned to Britain. Under pressure from Germany, Austria then offered Italy bribes in the form of some French territory and in addition the South Tyrol (which includes the Brenner Pass) and a shift in Italy's eastern frontier toward but not including Trieste and the Adriatic island of Pelagosa. Meanwhile, deeming Austria's action against Serbia in late July 1914 offensive, hence incompatible with the terms of the Triple Alliance, undertaken moreover without consulting her, and implying augmented Austrian hegemony over the Balkans, Italy broke the Alliance and on 2 August officially announced her neutrality in the Great War.[1]

Italy's neutrality was her first contribution to Allied victory because she released for operations against Germany between 200,000 and 300,000 Frenchmen who had been guarding the Italo-French frontier and by holding on her front many Austrian soldiers who might have been used against Russia. Yet after she joined them Italy was to prove a burden to the Allies in several ways. She lacked iron, coal, cotton, and phosphates, and for wheat was in bondage to foreign lands. Her naval power was not impressive, and she intended to fight for her own rather than Allied objectives. While persistently demanding that the Allies strengthen her fleet, she insisted that all Allied ships lent that fleet be commanded by Italians.[1] Further, given the geography of the Adriatic, Austria enjoyed a strategic advantage that discounted Italy's superiority in ships and guns.

Despite previous Italian and Austrian guarantees

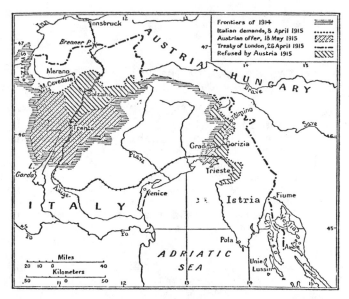

I. NEGOTIATIONS IN 1915: ITALIAN DEMANDS FROM AUSTRIA-HUNGARY, AUSTRIAN OFFER; TREATY OF LONDON

The lines in this map are taken from Temperley, *A History of the Peace Conference of Paris;* Toscano, *Il patto di Londra.*

René Albrecht-Carrié, <u>Italy at the Paris Peace Conference</u>. Hamden, Conn.: Archon Books, 1966, p. 23.

II. NEGOTIATIONS FOR THE TREATY OF LONDON IN THE ADRIATIC: ITALIAN
DEMANDS, OFFER OF THE ENTENTE

The lines in this map are taken from Toscano, *Il patto di Londra*.

René Albrecht-Carrié, Italy at the Peace
Conference. Hamden, Conn.: Archon Books,
1966, p. 27.

of Albania's independence, Italy would deny the use of Valona harbor to any other foreign power by seizing and fortifying the island of Saseno, which dominated its entrance. She would also guard the passage through the narrow Otranto Strait. On 25 October 1914 she established a blockade of the Albanian coast, on the thirtieth occupied and began to fortify Saseno island, and in December occupied Valona. These actions appeared to be of great help to the Allied side, but Italy now had to keep communications open across the Adriatic, thus offering Austria an additional line along which to strike her.[3]

The Great War made the Adriatic a battleground between Austrian and Anglo-French naval forces, with the ensuing naval blockade and counterblockade affecting Italy because both sides laid mines and 80 percent of Italy's trade went by sea. On 14 August 1914, Adm. Boué Lapeyrère, with British and French ships, raised the Austrian blockade of Montenegro. Yet Lapeyrère never mounted a joint operation to seize the much more important port of Cattaro and, after 3 November, because of enemy submarines and hydroplanes, heavy Allied ships retired to Otranto Strait, leaving the escort of convoys to Montenegro to destroyers.[4]

Deadlock on the Western Front was then matched by that on the Adriatic Sea, whose geography dictated naval strategy for both Austria and Italy. Except for Venice and Brindisi, the Italian Adriatic coast for the 850 kilometers between the Tagliamento River and Santa Maria di Leuca lacks natural shelters and anchorages and even adequate artificial ports, and can easily be bombarded from the sea. Venice was too restricted to maintain large numbers of ships and was poorly defend against all but small craft, Porto Corsini could sustain only light craft, and Ancona had such a poor anchorage that on 14 December 1914 Italy proclaimed her an open city. Brindisi was large enough to hold the entire Italian fleet, but its defenses were very inadequate, and it needed additional dredging to permit is use by major warships. As for aircraft, in August 1914 Italy had fourteen hydroplanes of fourteen different makes. Thereafter her aircraft manufacturers could not keep up with Army demands let alone those of the Navy.[5]

Italy used light craft for local defense and held her major ships ready for battle with the Austrian fleet. When Austria, however, retained her

THE ITALIAN FRONT

THE BALKAN AND ITALIAN FRONTS

SMALL CALIBER FLOATING BATTERIES

fleet as a fleet-in-being, Italy have up her plan of seeking decisive offensive action in favor of a policy of slow and methodical attrition except for trying to occupy some islands lying off the Dalmatian coast and some territory on that coast.[6]

In contrast to Italy's Adriatic coast, the Austrian Dalmatian coast provided a "mariner's paradise": the magnificent ports and naval bases of Trieste, Fiume, Pola, Zara, Sebenico, Spalato, and Cattaro served Austrian surface ships and submarines and German U-boats as well. Pola dominated Venice, and Austrian ships could strike Italian naval or merchant ships or Italy's coast and retire to safety in numerous littoral bases. To counter the main Austrian fleets, at Pola and Cattaro, Italy had to divide her fleets between Venice and Brindisi, with the ships at Venice also supporting the Italian army's drive eastward along the Gulf of Trieste. Italy's battleships remained at Taranto, where they could join the French squadron at Corfu if the Austrian fleet tried to leave the Adriatic.

Austria had some disadvantages. She could not operate in the Mediterranean because her light ships lacked sufficient range and she had no intermediate port south of Cattaro or on the Middle Sea; Italy had seized Valona; and British and French ships blocked the Strait of Otranto. In consequence on 1 August 1914, Hungary's military chieftain, the Archduke Frederick, directed Adm. Anton A.H. Haus to limit his efforts to the defense of the Adriatic. Haus concentrated his battle fleet at Pola and awaited Italian attacks while Italy chose to neutralize and blockade. Most important would be a net and mine barrage at the Strait of Otranto that would put a cork in the Adriatic bottle. Unfortunately for Italy, action on the Serbo-Montenegrin front made the occupation of the Island of Curzola and of the Sabbioncello Peninsula guarding Cattaro impossible.

Early in April 1915 Gen. Luigi Cadorna, head of the army, and Adm. Paolo Thaon di Revel, head of the navy, corresponded about how the navy could help the army advance toward Trieste. Di Revel could not guarantee protection of the littoral road to be used by the army unless he controlled the sea, a control that depended upon his defeat of an Austrian fleet that would not leave its superbly defended bases and accept battle. All he could do was to adopt attrition tactics.[7]

On 23 May 1915, the day Italy declared war on Austria, di Revel sent ships to stations along the mid Adriatic t and others to block Otranto Strait and to patrol from the Strait along the eastern Adriatic coast as far north as Cattaro. While ships from Venice attacked Porto Buso and Grado and cut the telegraph cable between Grado and Cittanova, others from Brindisi would destroy submarines and their bases in the Gulf of Brin and also seize the island of Pelagoza. Except for destroying the military works at Porto Buso, none of these objectives was obtained, and on the afternoon of the twenty-fourth the small destroyer <u>Turbine</u> was lost in an encounter with Austrian forces.[8] Meanwhile Admiral Haus sent three battleships, two cruisers, and various destroyers and torpedo boats out of Pola. These attacked fourteen Italian ports and the coastal railroad from Venice to Brindisi and so gained time for Austrian troops to reach Italy's frontier. By noon of the twenty-fourth his ships had retired and silence returned to the Adriatic. The Italians reacted by sending out raids to entice him out to sea--without success. Both sides then undertook attrition tactics by use of mines, small boats, submarines, and aerial action.[9]

The Italian navy's mission to support the army's drive from Venice to Trieste is clearly divided by the period before and after October 1917, or the Battle of Caporetto. For his first eleven battles of the Isonzo--counting Caporetto as the twelfth--Cadorna originally gained a few miles of territory and then was forced back. Fortunately for him, during the seventh through ninth battles in the autumn of 1916 Germany was engaged in the Verdun and Somme operations in the West and Brusilov offensive in the east and could provide Austria no help.

In the first period, in addition to defending littoral areas, the Italian navy provided the right with of Cadorna's army with naval guns and their crews, armed pontoons and monitors for bombarding land targets, ships to counter an attack by the Austrian fleet, and riflemen who provided the nucleus for what became a naval regiment ashore. However, Italy could not control of the Gulf of Trieste as long as the Austrian fleet remained at Pola. A second problem was that Italian ships must sail only behind minesweepers and remain almost immobile in order to lay their guns on land targets. However, in addition to laying mines to protect Venice, the navy forwarded logistic support to Cadorna via two internal canals dug to the east and west of the Tagliamento. Last, by October 1915 ninety-seven naval guns of various calibers had been sited between Porto Lignano and Monfalcone. In this way the army was provided better and more continuous gunfire support than could have been delivered by ships alone.[10]

Austrian naval inactivity in the Gulf of Trieste did not extend to other areas of the northern Adriatic. As early as 26 May 1915 a U-boat fired torpedoes at Italian ships at Venice; on 10 June the U-11 torpedoed and sank the Italian submarine _Medusa_ off the Lido; and on 10 July the cruiser _Amalfi_ was also torpedoed, in this instance by the U-4, a German boat out of Pola that still carried her German crew. Unceasing mine warfare was carried out by both sides, with Italy laying 12,293 mines in the gulfs of Venice and Trieste during the war and the Austrians 5,496.[11] With respect to aircraft and dirigibles, Austria's were more numerous and better equipped than Italian ones at the beginning of the war, and throughout 1915 the few Italian aerial operations undertaken proved ineffective. Both sides had quickly established a pattern of attack and counterattack on the other's air bases especially on moonless nights.[12]

Some U-boats out of Pola and Cattaro operated in the Mediterranean, and although Germany was not yet at war with Italy the boats left neither Italian nor other neutral ships immune from attack. On 7 November 1915 the U-39 took more than 200 lives, some of them American, when it sank the _Ancona_ and, a few days later, the _Firenze_. Tonnage sunk in November was four times greater than that of September, and Italy was also put to the task of sweeping German mines. In this endeavor she was aided by some French motorized fishing craft called _chalutiers_ and by some similar British drifters, but even those were not enough. Italy therefore had both private and public shipyards build a prototype A/S ship. But not until 1917 were twenty-seven RD boats produced, an inadequate number. The much larger _motoscafi antisommergibili_ (MAS) program, however, began to provide boats by mid 1916. Meanwhile 57mm or 74mm guns were provided to 948 merchant ships.[13]

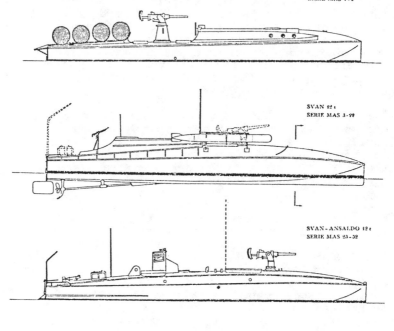

MAS TIPO "A"

SVAN 12 t pm.
SERIE MAS 1 - 2

SVAN 12 t
SERIE MAS 3 - 22

SVAN - ANSALDO 12 t
SERIE MAS 23 - 52

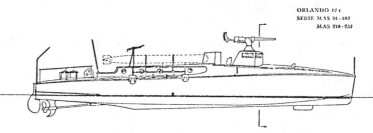

ORLANDO 12 t
SERIE MAS 91 - 102
MAS 218 - 232

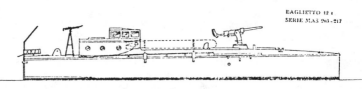

BAGLIETTO 12 t
SERIE MAS 203 - 217

S. Ten. di Vase. Erminio Bagnasco, "Lo sviluppo
e l'impiego dei Mas nella prima guerra mondiale,"
Rivista Marittima 98 (June 1965):70-71

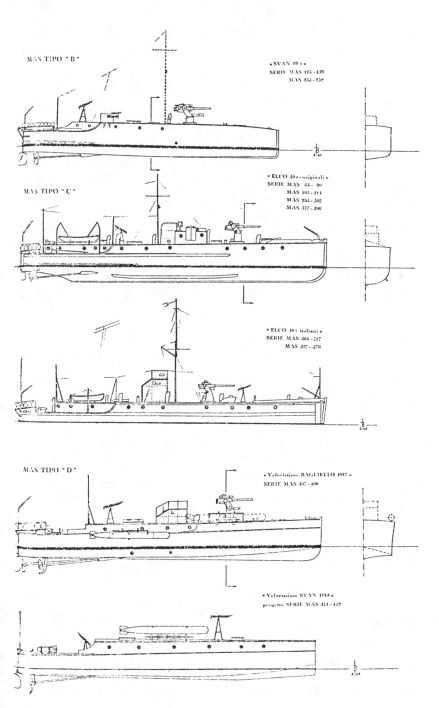

MAS TIPO "B"

«SVAN 49 »
SERIE MAS 115 - 139
MAS 233 - 252

MAS TIPO "C"

«ELCO 40 t - originali »
SERIE MAS 63 - 90
MAS 103 - 114
MAS 253 - 302
MAS 377 - 396

«ELCO 40 t italiani »
SERIE MAS 303 - 247
MAS 327 - 376

MAS TIPO "D"

«Velocissimo BAGLIETTO 1917 »
SERIE MAS 397 - 400

«Velocissimo SVAN 1918 »
progetto SERIE MAS 411 - 422

The advent of the U-boat in the Adriatic centered the attention of Allied naval leaders upon Otranto Strait, which is from 300 to 500 fathoms deep and twice as wide. Though it is tideless, violent storms are common there in winter. The only answer to U-boat transits of it seemed to lie with a surface bar- rage similar to the one at Dover. On 26 September 1916 British, French, and Italian small craft under British command began a permanent round-the-clock patrol of nets shot out between Cape Otranto and Saseno Island, near Valona. Held together by weak links that parted when a U-boat pushed them, the nets enveloped the boat and revealed its presence by agitating the glass globes that suspended them and setting off smoke bombs attached to the nets. Impeded in its movement, the boat must surface and could be destroyed either by gunfire or depth charge. Although better nets were employed, the barrage remained inefficient until the last year of war; throughout the war it probably claimed only three boats.[14]

Late in 1915 Britain, France, and Italy divided the Mediterranean into eighteen A/S zones: four for Italy, four for Britain, and ten for France. Little could be done about Austrian U-boats, however, as they lay in ambush in the Adriatic, as proved by torpedoes fired at the destroyers Dardo and Borea on 12 October 1915, the British cruiser Amethyst on the eighteenth, and the cruiser Dublin on 8 November. All missed. Moreover, on 27 September a terrific explosion had destroyed the battleship Benedetto Brin, with heavy loss of life. Investigation showed that the explosion had been caused by Italian-speaking Austrian sabateurs.[15] With her loss, the Minister of the Navy offered his resignation. He was succeeded by Adm. Camillo Corsi, who also accepted the resignation of the Chief of staff, di Revel, and assumed his duties. Similarly, the loss of French ships to U-boats provoked the dismissal in October of Admiral Lapeyrère and his replacement by Adm. Dartige du Fournet.

On 29 December 1915 occurred one of the rare meetings of Italian and Austrian surface ships. During the night of the twenty-eighth, the cruiser Helgoland and five destroyers out of Cattaro sank the French submarine Monge lying off the port of Durazzo, Albania. At 0600 the following morning the Austrian ships entered the port. Finding no enemy warships there, they retired, but while so

A MAS OF THE "53-62" SERIES UNDER WAY
Rivista Marittima 98 (June 1965):78

doing two destroyers hit mines, with one sinking and the other taken under tow. As cover, at 1150 the cruiser <u>K.Karl VI</u> escorted by three destroyers left Cattaro. To counter, at 0730 on the thirtieth British and Italian cruiser-destroyer forces left Brindisi. With their superior speed, however, the Austrians escaped. While two Austrian destroyers had been sunk, the Allies had lost a submarine and let slip an opportunity of destroying the entire Austrian force sent out from Cattaro.[16]

The first year of the war in the Adriatic thus passed without a meeting of major naval forces. If Austrian naval and aerial units raided the Italian coast and airfields, the Italian navy continued to wear the enemy out with small craft operations, supported the Italian army's drive toward Trieste, resupplied and strengthened Valona, destroyed enemy ships found along Dalmatian channels, and defended the Italian coast against hit and run raids.

When German guns opened fire upon Verdun on 7 February 1916, Cadorna undertook his Fifth Battle of the Isonzo in part to pin down Austrian troops and prevent their being transferred to the French Front. But by this time, according to Sir Maurice Hankey, Secretary of the Committee on Imperial Defence, "The Italians . . . felt a little out in the cold."[17] He was right. The British and French adopted a condescending attitude toward Italy because they saw her as a latecomer to the Allied cause and one who concentrated almost exclusively against Austria and gave little thought to the French Front. Of the Allied leaders, only French Prime Minister Aristide Briand had visited Italy. Italians had not been invited to the numerous Anglo-French conferences already held, and there was no liaison among the three countries.

To rectify this situation and improve relations, Cadorna visited London in March 1916 and Prime Minister Herbert Asquith accepted his invitation to visit Rome and the Italian army. On 3 April a British party lunched with the King in Udine, toured the front beyond the Tagliamento, and dined with Cadorna. April 4 was devoted to the Isonzo front. No real business was accomplished, yet the visit demonstrated to the Italians that the British were closely interested in their fortunes and gave Asquith opportunity to size up Italy's civil and military leaders.[19] It was clear, at least to the British writer K.G.B. Dewar, that "The Adriatic theatre remains an object-

MAP SHOWING THE AUSTRO-HUNGARIAN
FRONTIER ON THE DALMATIAN COAST

101

lesson in the weakness of naval and military allian-ces." [19]

The major cause of the Adriatic problem was less in numbers of ships than in the refusal of Italians to let foreigners command those of own ships that cooperated with theirs and the fact that Italy, not yet at war with Germany, could do nothing to counter German U-boats attacking Allied ships in the Mediterranean. These boats, however, caused the Allies to exchange views and concert measures on the conduct of the A/S war. In the spring of 1916 patrol zones were reassigned, Mediterranean shipping routes were regularized, intelligence and counter-espionage services were organized, and thought was given to stopping the use of Cattaro by Austrians. As long as the problem of Cattaro remained unsolved, Italy concentrated upon establishing the mine barrage at Otranto and shifted construction from four bat-tleships to fast cruisers that could counter destroy-ers and large numbers of small craft and aircraft. [20]

The greatest glory gained by Italian warships fell to the MAS. The original models displaced ten tons, were fifty-two feet long, and had a beam of ten feet and a draft of less than three feet. They could fire torpedoes, strike enemy coastal defense, and lay mines. The first two began operating on 6 June 1916, and on 1 July Italy ordered larger num-bers of them built. [21] Another development which proved very useful in coastal defense was armed trains. Carrying four 152s or 120s and usually two AA 76s, they had their own fire control cars, muni-tions cars, and locomotives at each end. Each train, which had a speed of about eighty kilometers per hour, was given a sixty kilometer section to guard from a station near the center of the zone. Ten such trains covered the Adriatic littoral from Venice to Brindisi. [22]

As in 1915 so in 1916, the Italian navy carried out surface, underwater, and aerial warfare and sup-ported the army. At the end of August 1916, the army called for even greater naval aid in what be-came the seventh, eighth, and ninth battles of the Isonzo. In these battles, naval barges carrying 203mm guns were particularly active. At request, moreover, the British sent the monitor <u>Earl of Peterborough</u>, which carried two 305s (12-inch) and some 76mm AA guns. She arrived in Venice just as the beginning of the winter season precluded army

PATROL AREAS
IN THE
MEDITERRANEAN

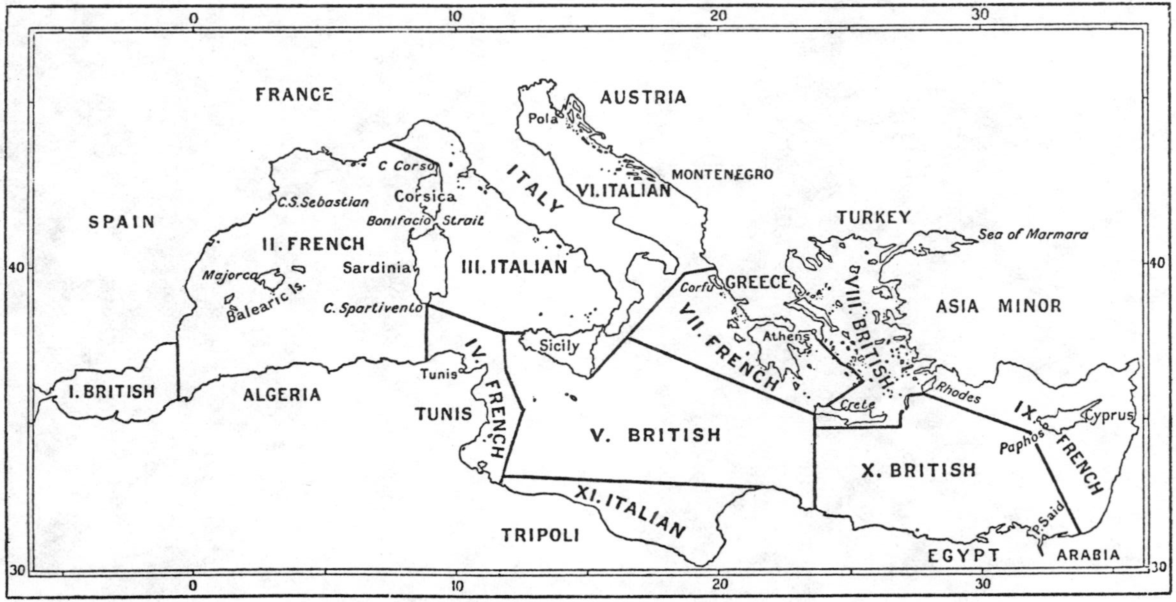

RAILWAY GUN OF 152mm IN POSITION.

ARMED TRAIN IN ACTION AGAINST ENEMY TORPEDO BOATS

operations.[23]

Truly exciting ventures were the penetration of enemy ports by Italian torpedo boats. On the night of 28 May 1916 Lt. Manfredi Gravina, with Nazario Sauro, an Austrian deserter, as pilot, entered the Gulf of Trieste. The two torpedoes fired merely hit a coal quay behind which lay merchant ships, but the boats made it back to Grado.[24] Then, on 7 June, several MAS entered Durazzo harbor and torpedoed an Austrian transport. On 2 November, in the most daring episode to date, MAS 20 entered Fasana Channel, an approach to Pola, and fired torpedoes at an old 7,400-ton ship being used as a school for junior officers. The torpedoes either became entangled in protective torpedo nets or failed to explode. As the Austrians learned next day, they were defective. In any event, the Italians returned unharmed to Venice. There had been absolutely no enemy reaction to their attack, and Austrian morale sank while Italian morale soared.[25]

If little change occurred in the war in the northern Adriatic in 1916, great changes occurred in the south after Austria obtained control of the Dalmatian coast from Cattaro southward, including the anchorages at Antivari and of S. Giovanni di Medua and of the port of Durazzo. In this southern region occurred the rescue of the Serb army, which by 15 October had disintegrated under Bulgar attacks. If rescued, the Serbs could be reformed and sent to join the Allied army at Salonika commanded by French Gen. Maurice Sarrail. Those Serbs who survived winter weather, hunger, disease, and death in Albania's mountains reached the Adriatic coast. From 22 December 1915 to 5 April 1916, while food and supplies came from Britain and France, which also supplied some transports, mostly Italian ships took the Serb soldiers, civilian refugees, and the many Austrian prisoners they had taken from Albania and delivered them to designated Italian ports, Marseilles, Corsica, or Corfu. By 10 February 1916 a hundred thousand men had been evacuated, and between 27 February and 5 April the last men and horses were embarked. At the cost of one Italian cruiser, one destroyer, and one drifter, five British drifters, and one French destroyer and two submarines the Allies had moved 260,895 persons, 10,153 horses, sixty-eight cannons, and some war materials. Of the 248 trips made, Italian flag ships made 151. Italy had voluntarily assumed the heaviest and most

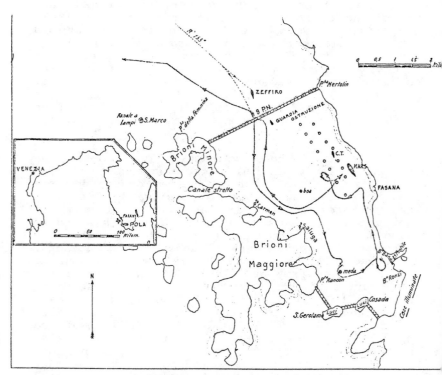

TRACK SHART OF THE OPERATION OF MAS No. 20
IN FASANA CHANNEL, 2 NOVEMBER 1916

duty to insure that no other nation acquired pre-
ponderance in the Adriatic.[26]

To destroy enemy traffic sailing at night
between defended ports along the Dalmatian coast,
early in 1916 Italian naval leaders restudied plans
for taking Lagosta, Pelagosa, or Gargano, or perhaps
the Sabbioncello Peninsula or northern coast of the
island of Curzola. When Cadorna said he would not
spare troops for such operations, the plans were
filed. Yet the improved strategic situation that
would result from the success of such operations was
so obvious that it attracted the attention especially
of France. When Admiral Dartige visited Taranto and
offered ships to the Italian fleet commander, the
Duke of Abruzzi, however, the Duke replied that
Italian ships were unavailable, adding the more important reason that any naval operation in the
Adriatic must be undertaken mostly by Italian ships
and troops.

Another tragic accident, very similar to that
of the Benedetto Brin, caused the loss of the battleship Leonardo da Vinci on 2 August in Taranto Harbor.
The court of inquiry held on the accident ruled out
unstable powder and suggested either negligence or
evil intent. It was later learned that the fire had
been started by enemy counteragents.

The Otranto net barrage was ineffective even
at the end of 1916 because of the lack of sufficient
defending ships and aircraft. The barrage also was
subject to sporadic Austrian raids. On 23 June 1916
the Italians lost the light cruiser Citta de Messina,
the French the destroyer Fource, and on 10 July the
Italians lost the destroyer Impetuoso. The cruiser-
destroyer patrols were therefore stopped, and the
barrage was moved southward, farther away from the
enemy's base at Cattaro. On 22 December, four Austrian destroyers attacked some of the trawlers and
drifters at Otranto while German U-boats freely
transited the strait on the surface.[27]

During the first eighteen months of the war,
then, major Italian naval operations included supporting and covering the Third Army's progress
from Venice toward Trieste, blockading the Austrian
and Albanian coasts, and driving Austrian ships
from the eastern Adriatic into inland canals. In
addition they established and defended the Otranto
Strait barrage, defended Italy's east coast, hunted

U-boats, kept heavy ships ready for a fleet action, laid and swept mines, exchanged submarine and aerial attacks with the Austrians, and built up aerial forces to equal those of Austria. Because of the Italian army's inability to spare troops, forward bases on Dalmatian islands or territory were not obtained. Unable to entice the Austrian fleet out to fight, have having lost two cruisers and two submarines to U-boats, cruisers and destroyers on the Otranto Barrage, and two battleships to Austrian sabateurs, the Italian navy continued to follow the principle of calculated risk, which meant that most operations devolved upon small craft, submarines, and aircraft.

Austrian surface ships remained like imprisoned beasts in their harbors for most of 1917 because they were inferior to the combined French and Italian forces. The unrestricted German U-boat campaign begun in February, however, became increasingly formidable by summer, when the Allies had not as yet devised adequate countermeasures. On 30 October 1916 British, French, and Italian naval commanders had conferred on how to improve the Otranto Strait Barrage. Their decision to move the northernmost line of drifters north to the Cape of Otranto so that fewer ships could guard a narrower passage proved unwise, for it attracted several Austrian attacks. Meanwhile Adm. Vittorio Cerri was experimenting with a fixed rather than mobile net system that could be sunk ten meters below the surface of the water, and plans were drafted for laying a net and mine barrage between Fano and Corfu.[28]

So bad was Italy's situation in the winter of 1916-1917 that doubt arose about her ability to continue her land war even though from May 1915 to May 1917 she received 30,500,000 tons of imports. To improve the safety of ship traffic was the major item on the agenda of an interallied naval conference held at Corfu on 28 April-1 May 1917, although how to make the Otranto Barrage effective and how to destroy the U-boat base at Cattaro were also considered. The suggestion by British Admiral Mark Kerr that the French command the A/S war in the Mediterranean was looked upon by the Italian delegate as being another step in the continuous if veiled attempt of the British to have one of their admirals exercise command over all Allied forces in the that sea, yet the conferees agreed to arm many more merchant ships, coordinate intelligence services,

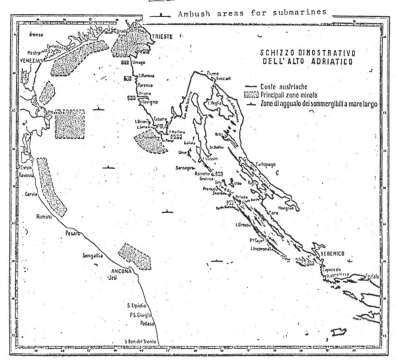

Austrian coasts

Principal mined zones

Ambush areas for submarines

SCHIZZO DIMOSTRATIVO
DELL' ALTO ADRIATICO

Coste austriache
Principali zone minate
Zone di agguato dei sommergibili a mare largo

Ufficio Storico della R. Marina, La Marina Italiana
nella Grande Guerra. Firenze: Vallechi Editore, 3:128

build more ships, and let the French create a general directorate for the U-boat war. However, Italian parochial policies prevented command in the Mediterranean from being given to the British.[29] On the other hand, while the institution of convoy would have made more efficient use of ships than patrolling, the Allies would not accept it; not until early 1917 did they agree that Italy could experiment with it. Just as Germany began her unrestricted U-boat campaign, Italy sent three convoys of three ships each out of Gibraltar, each with one destroyer escort. These reached Genova as safely as the troop transports being convoyed under escort to Albania and Salonika.[30]

Italy expected that the United States, once at war, would defend her own coasts, relieve the British and French of the burden of protecting seaborne traffic in the Atlantic and Pacific, and sent small A/S craft and troops across. Though she did not expect American help in the Mediterranean while the United States was not at war with Austria, she did hope that with American warships operating in the North Sea the British and French would be able to move some of their ships to the Mediterranean. Except for thirty-six submarine chasers, however, the United States would send no ships to the Middle Sea.

With the resumption of Germany's unrestricted U-boat war on 1 February 1917, David Lloyd George called for an interallied conference that would determine how Allied naval forces would be used in the Mediterranean. Among the agenda items of greatest interest to Italy were: 1) Operations that could be undertaken in the Adriatic, and 2) Britain's desire to disarm the four battleships she had sent to Italian waters and transfer the guns to new construction. Italy demanded that the battleships remain to counter the Austrian fleet and asked for twelve destroyers in addition to the twelve the French had promised in May 1915. In addition they wanted agreement reached upon Franco-Italian command relationships, the provision of a hundred more A/S craft at Otranto Strait, improved AS measures, and many more merchant ships to bring her coal, grains, and war supplies. Were the last not provided, she must close her factories and shipyards by March and soon thereafter cease military operations. To most of the demands the Allies agreed.[31]

The conferees also agreed that while for the moment it was impossible to conduct operations in

110

grande stile," minor operations should be pressed vigorously. When London insisted upon disarming the four battleships she has sent Italy, the French sent replacements for them--but the Italians would agree to French command only if the major part of the French fleet entered the Adriatic. Yet little attention was given to the Otranto Barrage, and the situation improved only a bit after Commo. Murray Sueter operated No. 6 Wing of the RNAS out of Taranto, for his planes were too few, his bombs too weak to be a real check to U-boats, and his torpedo planes failed to lift from the water. In return for the cruisers she now returned home, Britain sent six small reconnaissance dirigibles but not the direly needed destroyers she had promised Italy at the end of 1916.[32]

Because of the loss of the Leonardo da Vinci and the incompatibility of the naval chief of staff and minister of marine, Italian naval administration was reformed at the end of 1916. Di Revel, who had served as naval chief of staff from 1913 to 1915 and then commanded the Venice sector, was recalled to head the staff, and the aggressive fleet commander, the Duke of Abruzzi, was superseded by the cautious Adm. Rendina Cutinelli. Di Revel's strategy continued to be to "hold" until he acquired additional forces and meanwhile "hit" Austria with light ships, submarines, and aircraft. The leaders of the Austrian navy also changed in 1917, but their policy did not. Therefore both Italy and Austria continued to follow the principle of the calculated risk.

To support the italian army's drive against Trieste, on 22 March 1917 the Sir Thomas Picton joined her sister monitor and operated with two large and four small Italian monitors, all under Italian direction. At Taranto, meanwhile, a thousand-meter section of the anchored net barrage designed by Admiral Cerri had been laid more than ten meters below the surface of the water and after two months was hauled up undamaged. Yet it contained no explosives. Simultaneously, the French developed an explosive net system which floated near the surface. What was needed was to put the two systems together--but this would take time.[33]

Late in April 1917 Austria's Capt. Nicholas Horthy sent four motor torpedo boats (MTBs) to raid the Otranto Barrage, and three destroyers on the nights of 21-11 and 25-26 April and 5-6 May. Though little damage was done, Italians saw the raids as preliminary to a larger operation but could not predict its timing. On the evening of 14 May Horthy sortied from Cattaro with sixteen surface ships, three submarines, and twelve aircraft. Italy countered with twenty-one surface ships, two submarines, and thirteen aircraft. One group of Austrian ships sank a destroyer and two steamers in a convoy off Valona and damaged a third; they then began their return to base. A second group sank fourteen of the forty-seven drifters at Otranto and then made for Cattaro. Italian, French and British cruiser-destroyer forces that pursued had one light cruiser immobilized by a shell that cut her main steam line but damaged a destroyer and seriously wounded Horthy. However, with their superior speed the Austrians were able to make progress toward Cattaro. In a second group out of Brindisi, Adm. Alfred Acton had twenty ships to five Austrian. However, when the latter sent out the heavy cruiser Sankt George escorted by destroyers, he opened distance and ended the action. The Austrians towed their damaged Novara to Cattaro while the Dartmouth, although torpedoed, was also able to reach port under tow. On the other hand, the French destroyer Boutefue hit a mine and sank. The Austrian ships had fired more than twice the number of shells the Allies had and gained a decided success. Though no one divined the fact, the action would be the last major surface action to the end of the war.[34]

In February 1917 Archduke Karl Francis Joseph, Austria's new emperor, voiced his desire for peace to Britain, and in March to France, but his peace offering excluded Italy, to whom he would grant no territory. He would thus deny the demands for self-determination by Italy's irredenti which the Allies had promised Italy in the Treaty of London of 1915. If Karl failed in his attempt to obtain peace, so did Matthias Erzberger, a leader of the German Center party, who obtained from the Reichstag a resolution favoring a peace without annexations reminiscent of Wilson's "peace without victory" speech of January 1917 and much like the Pope's peace note issued on 1 August --all of which Germany's military authorities refused to accept.[35]

In the Mediterranean as well as in British waters, U-boat sinkings decreased during the summer and fall of 1917, especially after the Allies adopted

ITALIAN MONITOR TYPE A: THE CAPPELLINI

THE BRITISH MONITOR, SIR THOMAS PICTON

The Grillo (Cricket)

OPERATIONS OF MAS

First phase of the sinking of the Szent Istvan

Last phase

convoy, yet neither Britain nor the United States would send Italy the destroyers she said were needed.

In the meantime Italians built more aircraft, continued their experiments with A/S nets, to which they now added a number of mines provided by the French, ordered built another hundred MAS, and supported their Third Army. Work was also begun on a new type of boat, the <u>Grillo</u> (<u>Cricket</u>) on June 1917; she was expected to enter service in mid 1918. If they gloated over their proclaiming on 3 June 1917 "the independence of all Albania" under their protection, Italians fumed when an accord for a constitution for Jugoslav state was signed by the President of the Serb Council, Nikola Pǎsić, and the President of the National Jugoslav Council, Anto Trumbić.

Both technical and political problems were taken up at an Allied naval conference held in Paris on 24 July 1917. While di Revel agreed to British command in the Mediterranean and was pleased to learn that his allies would send him all the weapons they could spare for operations in the Adriatic to be decided upon, he countered excitedly when criticized for acting defensively rather than offensively against the Austrians. He was placated, and the conference ended on a cooperative note. Di Revel also agreed with a British plan to greatly extend the Otranto Barrage.[36]

At the interallied naval conference held in London on 4-5 September, the Italian representatives again asked for American aid, noting that while Britain had 375 destroyers and was being helped by the United States and Japan, Italy had only forty-one, twenty-one of which were obsolete. Further, Italy lacked materials with which to build new ones. Jellicoe thereupon sent six Australian destroyers which were at Malta, three submarines, and also two sections of the fixed mine barrage for Otranto, each 2,000 meters long, to which Italy added a similar section. The two and a half miles of net laid on October and early November was broken into three parts and the nets were hopelessly entangled by severe storms by the end of November. A better barrage must wait.[37]

With the Gen. Robert Nivelle campaign on the Western Front resulting in disaster and mutiny pervading the French army, her Western Allies said they could spare Italy only a hundred heavy guns. Lloyd George instead sent three hundred, but because of insufficient ammunition Cadorna could make no great impression against the enemy, now strengthened by six German divisions and artillery the Kaiser sent to attack "faithless Italy." At the end of August Cadorna postponed another offensive until May 1918. With Russia was now out of the reckoning, Germany and Austria shifted some of their best divisions from east to west.

With Britain alone continuing to fight on land and sea, Germany held on the Western Front and Austria hit Italy. The Battle of Caporetto belongs to the history of the land campaigns, but because it had a cathartic effect upon the Allies its main aspects deserve mention. The rout of the second of Cadorna's four armies stopped not at the Tagliamento but continued to the Piave. Fortunately, Cadorna had prepared defenses which now made it possible to cover Venice, only a few miles to the westward. He thus saved the Italian navy from moving down about five hundred miles to the next good naval base at Brindisi and letting the northern Adriatic pass into Austrian hands. That navy also did all it could to cover and support the withdrawing army. Moreover, General Foch visited Cadorna to inspire him with his confidence and promised to send him six infantry division, to which the British added five. Most important, Caporetto forced the Western Allies to abandon their tunnel vision and see the Western Front in its full dimensions, with not only tactics to think about but interallied strategy and logistics as well.[39] On 4 November, at Rapallo, a few miles southeast of Genova, Lloyd George spoke with Premier Vittorio E. Orlando and Foreign Minister Sidney Sonnino. On the fifth a Supreme War Council was created, with Cadorna a member. He was succeeded by Gen. Armando Diaz. Though the Italians held on the Piave without aid, on 25 November four Allied divisions entered the lines and Italy could reorganize her armies. Having sent many of his light craft and naval personnel to support Cadorna's drive eastward and then to cover its withdrawal, di Revel now asked the Allies to send him at least twenty large destroyers. Though the latter were not forthcoming, Jellicoe sent Admiral Wemyss to investigate the Italian situation.[39]

The interallied naval conference held in Paris on 29 November 1917 may be called the first of its kind because political as well as naval figures attended. While he could send no destroyers, Adm. William S. Benson said he would send Italy some yachts and would see what he could about munitions and sheet steel for shipbuilding. Second, an Allied Naval Council was established. Now there would be a single naval as well as military front and all member nations must subordinate their particular objectives to the council's conclusions. On 10 December, moreover, after she declared war on Austria, the United States assured Italy that she would provide colliers, tankers, and machine guns--with merchant tonnage, patrol craft, guns, sheet steel, and American-built MAS to follow.[40]

The winter of 1917 was the beginning of the end for Austria. On the night of 9 December Lt. Luigi Rizzo took a MAS into Trieste harbor on silent electric motors. Cutting through the hawsers supporting an obstruction boom, on the next morning he torpedoed and sank the 5,600-ton battleship Wein.[41] Heavy Austrian ships from Trieste were held off by Italian ones while the sinking of the Breslau and damaging of the Goeben during their sortie from the Black Sea on 18 January 1918 provided a welcome relief to Allied naval forces operating in the eastern Mediterranean. Moreover, with Cattaro unable to repair the increased number of U-boats sent to the Adriatic, these had to use Pola, Trieste, and Fiume. During the spring of 1918 the number of boats operating, and their sinkings, dropped.[42]

On land, in mid June 1918, Italy repelled several attacks and left the Austrian army paralyzed. In July, discontent occurred on Austrian ships at Pola but was quickly suppressed. On 16 October, Austria was transformed into a federal state that granted full autonomy to its various nationalities, a situation that countered Italy's territorial and irredentist aspirations. General Diaz thereupon decided to attack across the Piave and hoped that the Italian navy would undertake offensive air, surface ship, and submarine operations. On the latter point he was disappointed. At meetings of the Allied Naval Council di Revel renounced offensive operations and cooperation with his allies in favor of supporting national objectives. Particularly dismayed was Admiral Sims, who had suggested a combined Allied operation to seize Cattaro, some Dalmatian territory, and various Adriatic islands. For this purpose the United States would provide ships and men trained in

117

amphibious warfare. Under no condition, retorted di
Revel, would he place his forces under foreign command; nor would he send his battleships at Taranto to
sea to face air or submarine attacks. Allied relations with Italy in consequence cooled.[43]

Under French direction, the fixed Franco-Italian
net barrage between Corfu and Fano Island was completed on 11 February 1918, its withstanding the
rigors of winter weather ending British objections
to the laying of the great barrage between Fano Island and Otranto. Work began on 15 April under surface ship protection, but no Austrian surface ships
sortied until the night of 8 June, when Rear Admiral
Horthy ordered four battleships, four light cruisers,
and eight destroyers to concentrate at Cattaro prior
to attacking the barrage. Two of the battleships and
their destroyer screen from Pola sailed southward
through the Dalmatian Archipelago during the night of
9 June. When they were off Premuda at about 0300 on
the tenth, they were sighted by Lt. Luigi Rizzo.
Rizzo used his slowest speed in order to reduce
engine noise and wake, passed ahead of the enemy, got
between the destroyers flanking the battleship Szent
Ist ván, and at a distance of 300 meters fired six
torpedoes. These hit the Szent Ist ván right in the
middle; she sank at about 0600. Rizzo's second
boat fired at the Tegethoff but missed. The other
Austrian ships thereupon retired to Pola and remained
in port to the end of the war.[44]

By 30 September, after five months of strenuous
work, the new Otranto barrage was completed and
U-boat attacks in the Mediterranean practically
ceased. But only when his allies planned to attack
Durazzo preparatory to establishing a base there
from which Gen. Franchet D'Esperey could be supported in a drive against Bulgaria did di Revel stir.
On 2 October, Italian and British cruisers and destroyers and some American submarine chasers bombarded
Durazzo in the last Allied naval action of any kind
in the Adriatic.[45] With Bulgaria's request for an
armistice granted on 30 October, the Allies could use
the roads and railroads that ran from her territory
to the capitals of Germany and Austria-Hungary. The
last work undertaken by the Allied Naval Council, in
Paris between 29 October and 4 November, was to prepare naval armistice terms for Germany and Austria.

Meanwhile the Grillo had become operational.
Displacing eight tons, ten meters long and with a

THE BALKAN AND ITALIAN FRONTS, SEPTEMBER
30, 1918, and NOVEMBER 11, 1918. While
the Italiân army pushed northward in
Albania toward Montenegro, French armies
drove northward on the east and Serbian
troops on the west toward Belgrade.

very shallow draft, it was fitted with electric motors, protected propellers, caterpillar treads that enabled it to cross over barriers, chain saws to slice through wood, and torpedo-dropping gear. It had a speed of five knots, range of about twenty miles, and crew of three. On the night of 13-14 May 1918 Capt. Mario Pellegrini and three volunteers left Punta Penda for Pola. The Grillo had chopped through the first four obstructions in about two and a half minutes for each. It was making for the fifth when a shell from an enemy guard boat severed the arm of the torpedoman, who was about to launch his torpedo at the battleship Radetsky. Pellegrini thereupon decided to sink the Grillo.[46]

In his armistice terms di Revel wanted all Austrian and German U-boats in the Adriatic and the bulk of the Austrian surface fleet turned over to Italy. In addition Austria must dismantle all her fortifications along the Adriatic, remove all under-water obstructions, sweep her mines, and permit Italy to occupy her naval bases. Except for reducing the number of ships Austria must surrender to Italy, the Allied Naval Council agreed. Moreover, Austria must concentrate and immobilize all her aircraft and merchant ships in stated locations and evacuate all occupied territory. These terms were acceptable to the Allied premiers, who on 30 October telegraphed them to Diaz and directed him to insure that Austria either accepted or refused them by midnight of 3 November.[47]

Austria's final naval tragedy was still to come. At 1400 on 30 October a MAS left Venice carrying a mignatta (leech), a navigable torpedo propelled by compressed air which carried two mines of negative buoyancy containing time fuses and battery-powered electromagnetic clamps. Riding her were two powerful swimmers, naval engineer Raffaele Rossetti and Med-ical Lt. Raffaele Paolucci, both dressed in inflated rubber suits and having only their heads above water. The mignatta arrived at the multiple barrage lines of Pola at 2218. With the light of dawn, the Italians at 0415 attacked a mine to the hull of the flagship, Viribus Unitis. They were taken aboard and greeted as friends because the flag flying from the ship was not Austrian, Austria having a few hours earlier turned over her mutinous fleet and the Pola base to a newly created Slav government. In time to clear the ship of personnel before she was blown up, the Italians told about their time bomb and were made prisoners.[48]

While various Austrian ships and naval bases were transferred to local Jugoslav committees, Trieste on 30 October proclaimed her Italianity. On 2 November, Italian ships entered her port while Italians in Fiume also asked Italy to send ships. Meanwhile, at Villa Giusti, near Padua, Austrian delegates accepted Italy's armistice terms. As put by Comdr. Charles R. Train, the American naval attaché in Rome, "With the landing of Italian naval forces at Trieste and the capture of Rovereto and Trento by Diaz's soldiers, the Italian Risorgimento reaches its spiritual fruition and completion."[49]

Since Allied ships had not cooperated with her during the closing days of the war, some of the armistice terms appeared unjust to Italy, "the victory." Particularly irritating was the provision that permitted the four allies to occupy Pola. However, in completed disregard of these terms and with commendable promptness, ships from Venice, Ancona, and Brindisi occupied all the ports, islands, and inlets on the Dalmatian shore assigned to Italy in the Treaty of London and planted the Italian flag there before the period of the armistice ended. When the Supreme War Council directed that the former Austrian ships be sailed to Corfu, Adm. Umberto Cagni took a squadron into Pola on 6 November and forced the Yugoslavs to haul down their flags from the Austrian ships. Americans at Sebbenico and Frenchmen at Cattaro forced compliance with similar orders.[50] Thus the Yugoslav dream of possessing a navy failed to materialize while Italy obtained most of what she had been promised in the Treaty of London. She had redeemed her land and obtained absolute dominion over the Adriatic.

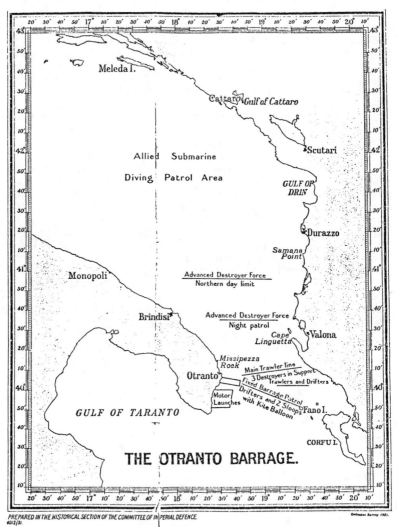

THE OTRANTO BARRAGE.

Meleda I.

Cattaro Gulf of Cattaro

Scutari

Allied   Submarine

Diving Patrol Area

GULF OF
DRIN

Durazzo

Samana
Point

Monopoli

Advanced Destroyer Force
Northern day limit

Brindisi

Advanced Destroyer Force
Night patrol

Cape
Linguetta

Valona

Missipezza
Rock

Main Trawler line

Otranto

3 Destroyers in Support
Trawlers and Drifters

Fixed Barrage Patrol

Motor
Launches

Drifters and 2 Sloops
with Kite Balloon

Fano I.

GULF OF TARANTO

CORFU I.

Julian S. Corbett and Henry Newbolt, History of the Great War
Based on Official Documents: Naval Operations, 5 vols. London:
Longmans, Green, 1920-1931, 5: end maps, Fog. 6.

SUMMARY AND CONCLUSIONS

As true earlier and later, Belgium, Greece, and Luxembourg proved the truth of the principle that a defenseless neutrality is an invitation to aggression. Second, all the powers engaged in the Great War were unprepared in the air, on the land, on the surface of the water and under it to fight the kind of war it turned out to be. The first war fought in three dimensions therefore called for the devising of doctrine for the offensive and defensive employment of new weapons in what in the end was a war of economic attrition.

British naval leaders well knew that the safety of their isles, their Empire, and of their allies as well rested upon their obtaining and exercising a command of the sea that would permit them to engage in overseas trade, transport troops wherever they were needed, and launch amphibious operations while interdicting enemy communications. With material superiority over Germany, British naval commanders could act aggressively while German leaders feared the loss of ships. In contrast to the fateful strategic consequences of the loss of the Grand Fleet, the loss of her "luxury fleet" would have had little strategic impact upon Germany's fortunes at war. A prime land power, she intended to win the war on land before naval forces could significantly affect its outcome. However, the long stalemate in trench warfare placed her at a great disadvantage. In time, Allied sea power redressed the considerable land strength of the Central Powers and the entry of the United States into the war more than compensated for Russia's defalcation.

Germany's naval strategy was to use the mine and torpedo to bring the Grand Fleet to approximate equality with the High Seas Fleet prior to seeking a pitched battle. Had the Allies possessed no submarines, they still could have won the war; had Germany possessed none, the war at sea probably would not have lasted a year.[1] Unable to use the High Seas Fleet to interdict Allied surface ships, Germany used U-boat warfare. The Allies retorted with escort of convoy and other measures. More important, that warfare was a prime reason the United States entered the war. Germany tried hard to force a decision on land in the spring of 1918, but the Allies were able to hold out until American reinforcements turned the tide in their favor. The Allied and American naval contribution was a vital ingredient in the ultimate outcome.

Many books have been written about "blunders" committed during the Great War. Among errors committed by the Central Powers were their failure to alert their steamers and cruiser raiders in time to prevent the internment of many of them in neutral ports, Germany's original lack of concern about the passage of the BEF to France, the Kaiser's order that the High Seas Fleet serve merely as a fleet-in-being, thus conceding to Britain command of the sea, and Germany's failure to acquire French ports located along the English Channel. Other mistakes were the small number of U-boats with which Germany began the war, and slowness in gauging their utility against merchant ships, the poor organization of the German naval high command, lack of joint army-navy plans, and absence of joint plans with Austria. Last, there was the poor timing of the unrestricted U-boat campaign beginning 1 February 1917, the latter's inability to wrest command of the sea from the Allies, and its provoking the United States into the war.

On the Allied side, blunders involved the lack of Anglo-Russian naval plans for a war against Germany, the British want of adequate policy-determing machinery at least to the end of 1916, and of a naval staff system, and indeed, of agreement upon naval objectives. In addition the British let the Goeben and Breslau escape, the Grand Fleet failed to destroy the High Seas Fleet at Jutland, and the Allies failed in their Gallipoli venture. The Allies may also be criticized for their failure to adopt the convoy system until the spring of 1917 and their pitting their strength against German strength on the Franco-Belgian Front rather than exploiting weaknesses on the Austro-Italian Front.[2]

Neutral nations had the alternatives of acquiescing to the British maritime control system or forcing its abandonment by diplomatic, military, or economic pressure. Bothersome as it was to the United States, complaints could be adjudicated peacefully and with profit to Americans, whereas the taking of American lives on belligerent ships by U-boats could not. Under American pressure, Germany gave up U-boat warfare except under prize rules for the year between February 1916 and February 1917. With its resumption, the United States entered the war. Like all other nations, however, she was unprepared for war. She had money and untapped material and manpower resources but was unready to fight an A/S war in three dimensions. Its naval organization was poor and it was very slow in providing Admiral Sims, commanding American naval forces in European waters, with the ships and staff he needed. Also, because war against Austria was not declared until December 1917, the United States failed to support Italy, one of the Allies, who was at war with Austria.

On the other hand, America's contributions sufficed to enable the Allies to overcome both the U-boats and the armies of the Central Powers. It lent the Allies $8 billion; by refusing exports to neutrals near Germany it greatly strengthened the economic blockade of Germany. It send across thirty-six of its modern destroyers, several destroyer tenders, more than three hundred small A/S craft, built several million tons of cargo and transport ships, provided sea lift for about half of the two million soldiers who went "over there," produced the revolutionary antenna mine that greatly reduced the number of mines for the North Sea Mine Barrage, and toward the end of the war had a fairly respectable military and naval aviation contingent overseas. Not to be overlooked is Admiral Sims, who so well advised Washington on what was needed to win the war, served well as a member of the Allied Naval Council, cooperated with General Pershing, and nudged the British to adopt the convoy system.

A brutal yet valid assessment of Italy's reasons for entering the war after a nine-month neutrality period include her desire to prove herself a Great Power, the Allies' promises to obtain secure frontiers for her and more territory than the Central Powers offered her--enough to make the Adriatic an Italian lake and to nationalize her _irredenti_ and thus bring the _Risorgimento_ to fruition. However, the geography of the Adriatic gave Austria a strategic advantage that discounted Italy's superiority in ships and guns. Moreover, Italy's lack of natural resources meant that she must depend for food, fuel, munitions, and shipping upon Allied sources.

As the British and Germans did in the North Sea, so in the Adriatic the Austrians and Italians kept their fleets in-being and resorted to using submarines, light ships, and aircraft for defensive and offensive purposes. Like Jellicoe, Italian naval leaders would not be led over mined or submarine infested wars. The impregnable ports of Pola and Cattaro were to Italy what Ostend and Zeebrugge were to the British. Unfortunately for Italy, her army, occupied in trying to reach Trieste from Venice, could never spare sufficient troops to seize and defend some Dalmatian islands or coastal territory. However, following its defeat by Bulgars and Germans, from November 1915 to April 1916 Italy provided the bulk of the sea lift, supplies, and food that rescued the Serb army. If, despite help from Britain and France, Italy never established a truly effective mine barrage at Otranto Strait until the very end of the war, its navy cooperated well in defense of the Italian army as it retreated from Caporetto.

In the Atlantic, the American and British navies cooperated; in the Mediterranean, British, French, and Italian leaders clashed. Nor did new command arrangements and the establishment of the Allied Naval Council smooth Allied naval relations and improve their operations in the Mediterranean and Adriatic seas, for the Italians rejected demands to adopt an offensive attitude and unity of command. It was evident that she was more interested in achieving her own objectives than in pooling her resources for the common good, and in the end she obtained most of what she wanted from Austria. For inventiveness and audacity, moreover, the Italians were supreme, as proved by the sinking of the Austrian battleships <u>Wein</u> and <u>Szent István</u> by mere MAS and of the <u>Viribus Unitis</u> by a <u>mignatta</u>.

While the British admitted that they had made mistakes during the war, they refused to reveal their dirty laundry to the world. Two committees of investigation eventually resulted in the creation of a Naval Staff College and of a Tactical School.[3] However, in a Congressional investigation in Washington in early 1920, Sims charged that the Navy Depart's poor organization and dilatory procedures for the first six months of the war had delayed victory by four months and cost the Allied cause 2.5 million tons of shipping, 500,000 lives, and $15 billion. With partisanship intruding, he failed to prove his case.[+]

Neither Allied land power nor Allied naval power alone won the war. Allied sea power transported British Imperial armies to the continent and protected and supplied them; destroyed German surface cruiser raiders; helped despoil Germany of her colonial empire; held the High Seas Fleet in check; and barely won its war against the U-boat in the first Battle of the Atlantic. Allied armies proved ineffective on the Western Front and at Salonika from 1915 to 1918 although Easterners could crow about successes in the Near East. To the generals, the naval war appeared subsidiary; it had not caused the downfall of a continental bloc as strong the Central Powers particularly after it was nurtured by Romanian and Russian oil and wheat and continued to enjoy good communications and the interior lines of position. Further, the battleship had been denied its utility by the U-boat. To the generals, then, the land campaign had forced the enemy to surrender. They were both right and wrong. The Allies won by a combined sea, land, and air blockade--with manpower and economic attrition visited upon the enemy armies by the pressure of the blockade by sea as well as by the Allied armies. In the end, Allied and American command of the seas permitted the transfer of men and resources from the United States that made possible the victory on land.

NOTES

The following abbreviations have been used:

ADM	Admiral
CAPT	Captain
CDR	Commander
COMMO	Commodore
GB	General Board of the Navy
GEN	General
GPO	Government Printing Office
HMSO	His Majesty's Stationery Office
LCDR	Lieutenant Commander
LT	Lieutenant
MA	Military Affairs
MDLC	Manuscript Division, Library of Congress
NARG	National Archives Record Group
ONI	Office of Naval Intelligence
RADM	Rear Admiral
RUSIJ	Royal United Service Institution Journal
SECNAV	Secretary of the Navy
USMC	U.S. Marine Corps
USNIP	U.S. Naval Institute Proceedings
VADM	Vice Admiral

CHAPTER 1

1. Statements of the functions of the British and German fleets, respectively, are found in John R. Jellicoe, The Grand Fleet. New York: George H. Doran, 1919, pp. 12-13, and ADM Scheer, Germany's High Sea Fleet. New York: Peter Smith, 1934, p. 25.

2. C. Ernest Fayle, Seaborne Trade: History of the Great War Based on Official Documents, 2 vols. New York: Longman's Green, 1920-1933, 1:1-57; Lord Hankey, The Supreme Command, 2 vols. London: George Allen and Unwin, 1961, 1:102; Gerd Hardach, The First World War, 1914-1918. Berkeley and Los Angeles: University of California Press, 1977.

3. Violet Bonham Carter, Winston Churchill: An Intimate Portrait. New York: Harcourt, Brace &

World, 1965, pp. 185, 191; Winston Churchill, The World Crisis, 4 vols in 1. New York: Charles Scribner's Sons, 1931, pp. 51-59; Leslie Gardiner, The British Admiralty. Edinburgh and London: William Blackwood & Sons, 1968, p. 318; Air Chief Marshal Sir Arthur Longmore, From Sea to Sky, 1910-1915. London: Geoffrey Bles, 1946, pp. 24, 25, 29-30, 34-46; Arthur J. Marder, "Winston Churchill as First Lord of the Admiralty, 1911-1915," USNIP 79 (Jan. 1953):1920.

4. Paul Kennedy, "Strategic Aspects of the Anglo-German Naval Race." In his Strategy and Diplomacy, 1870-1945: Eight Studies. London: Allen & Unwin, 1983, pp. 128-51.

5. CAPT Auguste A. Thomazi, French Navy, La Guerre navale dans la zone des armees du Nord. Paris: Payot, 1925, pp. 9-20, 27-31; Christophe M. Andrew, "France and the German Menace." In Ernest R. May, ed. Knowing One's Enemies: Intelligence Assessment before the Two World Wars. Princeton, N.J.: Princeton University Press, 1984, pp. 127-49, and Jan Karl Tanenbaum, "French Estimates of Germany's Operational War Plans," ibid., pp. 150-71.

6. Churchill, World Crisis, pp. 111-12; "The War: Its Naval Side," RUSIJ 60 (Nov. 1914):523.

CHAPTER 2

1. Martin Gilbert, Winston Churchill, 4 vols. Boston: Houghton Mifflin, 1919-1922, 3:18; George Kopp, Two Lone Ships: Goeben and Breslau. London: Hutchinson, 1931; Sir A. Berkeley Milne, The Flight of the 'Goeben' and 'Breslau.' London: Eveleigh Nash Co., 1921; Auguste Thomazi, CAPT French Navy, La Guerre navale dans l'Adriatique. Paris; Payot, 1925, pp. 7-20.

2. C.R.M.F. Cruttwell, A History of the Great War 1914-1918, 2d ed. Oxford: Clarendon Press, 1936, p. 65; Bernard Fitzsimon, ed, Warplanes and Air Battles of World War I. London: Phoebus, 1973, p. 276; Air Chief Marshal Sir Arthur Longmore, From Sea to Sky 1910-1915. London: Geoffrey Bles, 1946, pp. 39-40; Sir Walter

Raleigh and Henry Jones, <u>The War in the Air:</u> <u>Official</u> <u>History of the War, Based on Official</u> <u>Documents</u>, 6 vols. Oxford: Clarendon Press, 1922-1934, 1:357-409.

3. ADM Scheer, <u>Germany's High Sea Fleet in the</u> <u>World War</u>. New York: Peter Smith, 1934, pp. 63-64; Amiral [Raoul V.P.] Castex, <u>Theories</u> <u>Strategiques</u>. Vol. 2 Ch. 6. <u>The German Opera-</u> <u>tions in the North Sea (1914-1916)</u>. Trans. by LCDR Charles Moran, USNR. Stenciled and printed at the Naval War College, Newport, Rhode Island, Sept. 1932, p. 14.

4. Holger H. Herwig, <u>"Luxury Fleet": The Imperial</u> <u>German Navy 1888-1918</u>. London: George Allen & Unwin, 1980, pp. 160-1; Alfred Tirpitz, <u>My</u> <u>Memoirs</u>, 2 vols. New York: Dodd, Mead, 1919, 2:78-80, 88; Hugo Waldeyer-Hartz, <u>Admiral von</u> <u>Hipper</u>. Trans. by Appleby Holt. London: Rich & Cowan, 1933, pp. 108-12.

5. <u>London Times</u>, Aug. 28, Sept. 1, 1914; W. S. Chalmers, <u>The Life and Letters of David Beatty,</u> <u>Admiral of the Fleet</u>. London: Hodder & Stough-ton, 1951, pp. 134-55; Roger Keyes, <u>The Naval</u> <u>Memoirs of Admiral of the Fleet Sir Roger</u> <u>Keyes</u>, 2 vols. New York: E.P. Dutton, 1934-1935, 1:79-97.

6. Alan Coles, <u>Three Before Breakfast: A True and</u> <u>Dramatic Account of How a German U-boat Sank</u> <u>Three British Cruisers in One Desperate Hour</u>. Homewell, Havant, Hampshire: Kenneth Mason, 1979. A first-hand account is by LT. Johannes Spiess, <u>Six ans de crosiers en sousmarin</u>. Trans. from the German by Lt. Henry Schriek. Paris: Payot, 1929, pp. 45-61.

7. ADM Sir Reginald H. Bacon, <u>The Concise Story of</u> <u>the Dover Patrol</u>. London: Hutchinson, 1932, pp. 28-29; Violet Bonham Carter, <u>Winston Churchill:</u> <u>An Intimate Portrait</u>. New York: Harcourt, Brace & World, 1965, pp. 271-80; Lowell Thomas, <u>Raiders of the Deep</u>. Garden City, N.Y.: Doubleday, Doran, 1918, pp. 30-5.

8. ADM of the Fleet Fisher, <u>Memories and Records</u>, 2 vols. New York: George H. Doran, 1920, 2:97; Scheer, <u>Germany's High Sea Fleet</u>, pp. 69-72; Waldeyer-Hartz, <u>Hipper</u>, pp. 125-28, 132-36.

9. London Times, Jan. 1-4, 8, 1915; Julian S. Cor-
    bett and Henry Newbolt, History of the Great
    War, Based on Official Documents: Naval Opera-
    tions, 5 vols. London: Longmans, Green, 1920-
    1931, 2:64-66; Field Marshal Viscount French of
    Ypres, 1914. Boston: Houghton Mifflin, 1919, pp.
    317-18, 324-25.

10. CAPT Thomas G. Frothingham, USNR, The Naval
    History of the World War: The United States in
    the War 1917-1918, 3 vols. Cambridge, Mass.:
    Harvard University Press, 1924-1926, 1:229-39;
    A. Temple Patterson, Tyrwhitt of the Harwich
    Force: The Life of Admiral of the Fleet Sir
    Reginald Tyrwhitt. London: Macdonald, 1973, p.
    103; Scheer, Germany's High Sea Fleet, pp.
    77-80; Waldeyer-Hartz, Hipper, pp. 153-60.

11. Winston Churchill, The World Crisis, 4 vols. in
    1. New York: Charles Scribner's Sons, 1931, pp.
    271, 352; Roger Keyes, The Naval Memoirs of Ad-
    miral of the Fleet Sir Roger Keyes, 2 vols. New
    York: E.P. Dutton, 1934-1935, 2:36.

12. Reginald H. Bacon, The Life of Lord Fisher of
    Kilverstone, 2 vols. Garden City, N.Y.: Double-
    day, Doran, 1929, 2:187-94; Fisher, Memories
    and Records, 1:67; Trumbull Higgins, Winston
    Churchill and the Dardanelles: A Dialogue in
    Ends and Means. New York: Macmillan, 1964, p.
    15.

13. Bacon, Dover Patrol, pp. 30, 39-46, 86, 136,
    149; Fisher, Memories and Records, 1:68; ADM
    Sir Lewis Bayly, Pull Together: The Memoirs of
    Admiral Sir Lewis Bayly. London: George G.
    Harrap, 1939, p. 152.

14. George F. Abbott, Greece and the Allies, 1914-
    1922. London: Methuen, 1922, pp. 4-20; Mark
    Kerr, Land, Sea, and Air: Reminiscences of
    Mark Kerr. New York: Longmans, Green, 1927, pp.
    184-92.

15. Abbott, Greece and the Allies, pp. 21-27;
    Bacon, Dover Patrol, pp. 92-93; Carter, Chur-
    chill, p. 287; Churchill, World Crisis, p. 284;
    Lord Hankey, The Supreme Command, 2 vols. Lon-
    don: George Allen & Unwin, 1961, 1:245-51; Hig-
    gins, Churchill and the Dardanelles, pp. 102-5;
    David Lloyd George, War Memoirs of David Lloyd

George, 6 vols. Boston: Little, Brown, 1933-1937, 2:3-9.

16. Churchill, World Crisis, p. 306.

17. Carter, Churchill, p. 286.

18. Bacon, Fisher, 2:199-276; Carter, Churchill, pp. 290, 318-19, 211-33; Fisher, Memories and Records, 1:68-71; Hankey, Supreme Command, 1: 253-54, 269-84; Higgins, Churchill and the Dardanelles, pp. 103-6, 108, 113-15, 122-32; Keyes, Naval Memoirs, 1:178-79, 182; Lloyd George, Memoirs, 1:68-69, 343-44, 346-53.

19. Who Goes There? London: Hutchinson, 1942, p. 156.

20. Corbett and Newbolt, Naval Operations, 2:256.

21. Lloyd George, Memoirs, 1:422.

22. Philip Lundeberg, "Underwater Warfare and Allied Strategy in World War I. Part I," The Smithsonian Journal of History 1 (Autumn 1966): 1-9. See also Contrammiraglio Gino Gallupini (G.N.) [equivalent to Naval Constructor], "Nel Sessantesimo Anniversario dell' Invasione nei Dardanelli," Rivista Marittima 105 (July-Aug. 1977):173-94.

CHAPTER 3

1. Richard H. Gibson and Maurice Prendergast, The German Submarine War 1914-1918. New York: Richard R. Smith, 1931, pp. vii, 1, 5-13; VADM Andreas Michelsen, Ret., Formerly Commander Submarine Forces, The Submarine Warfare, 1914-1918. Trans. of Der U-Bootskrieg, 1914-1918. Washington: NARS, copy of original typescript in NARG 45; ADM Scheer, Germany's High Sea Fleet in the World War. New York: Peter Smith, 1934, p. 284; Philip K. Lundeberg, "The German Naval Critique of the U-boat Campaign, 1915-1918," MA 27 (Fall 19630;106. On the development of the submarine among others, see Don Everitt, The K-Boats: A Dramatic First Report on the Navy's Most Calamitous Submarines. New York: Rinehart & Winston, 1963.

2. Michelsen, Submarine Warfare 1914-1918, p. 15; Gibson and Prendergast, German Submarine War 1914-1918, p. 26; Scheer, Germany's High Sea Fleet, p. 284; Arno Spindler, "The Value of the Submarine Warfare," USNIP 52 (May 1926):830.

3. Gibson and Prendergast, German Submarine War 1914-1918, pp. 19-20; Archibald Hurd, The Merchant Navy: History of the Great War Based on Official Documents, 3 vols. London: John Murray, 1921-1929, 1:231-38. For details, see VADM Reginald H. Bacon, The Concise Story of the Dover Patrol. London: Hutchinson, 1932, and E. Keble Chatterton, Danger Zone: The Story of the Queenstown Command. Boston: Little, Brown, 1943, The Big Blockade. London: Hurst & Blackett, 1932, The Sea Raiders. London: Hurst & Blackett, 1931; The Auxiliary Patrol. London: Sidgwick & Jackson, 1923, and Q Ships and Their Story. London: Sidgwick & Jackson, 1922.

4. London Times, Aug. 4, 5, 25, Nov. 7, Dec. 23, 1914; Paolo E. Coletta, William Jennings Bryan: Progressive Politician and Moral Statesman, 1909-1915. Lincoln: University of Nebraska Press, 1969, pp. 266-67; Louis Guichard, The Naval Blockade, 1914-1918. New York: D. Appleton & Co., 1930, pp. 21-22.

5. Sir Edward Grey (Viscount of Fallodon), Twenty-five Years, 1892-1916, 2 vols. New York: Frederick A. Stokes, 1925, 2:107.

6. London Times, Nov. 10, 1914; C. Ernest Fayle, Seaborne Trade . . . , 3 vols. New York: Longmans, Green, 1920-1933, 2:9-10; Guichard, Naval Blockade, 1914-1918, pp. 37-39; Scheer, Germany's High Sea Fleet, pp. 216-17; Alfred Tirpitz, My Memoirs, 2 vols. New York: Dodd, Mead, 1919, 2:137-43.

7. Bryan to Gerard, Feb. 10, 1915, Papers Relating to the Foreign Relations of the United States, 1915. Supplement. Washington: Department of State, 1928, pp. 98-100.

8. Julian S. Corbett and Henry Newbolt, History of the Great War, Based on Official Documents: Naval Operations, 5 vols. London: Longmans, Green, 1920-1931, 2:45-49, 59, 121-28, 271-75, 385-87; Fayle, Seaborne Trade, 2:20, 96-98,

103-5, 148-97, 205-6, 218; Robert Lansing, <u>War Memoirs of Robert Lansing, Secretary of State</u>. New York: Bobbs-Merrill, 1935, pp. 43-52; Michelsen, <u>Submarine Warfare, 1914-1918</u>, pp. 19, 30; Daniel M. Smith, <u>Robert Lansing and American Neutrality 1914-1917</u>. Berkeley and Los Angeles: University of California Press, 1958, pp. 56-60.

9. <u>London Times</u>, mar. 29-31, Apr. 2, 9, 10, May 8, 1915; Lansing, <u>War Memoirs</u>, p. 32; Arthur S. Link, <u>Wilson: Campaigns for Progressivism and Peace, 1916-1917</u>. Princeton, N.J.: Princeton University Press, 1965, pp. 645-57.

10. Karl E. Birnbaum, <u>Peace Moves and U-Boat Warfare: A Study of Imperial Germany's Policy Toward the United States, April 8, 1916-January 9, 1917</u>. Stockholm: Almquist & Wiksell, 1958, pp. 27-32; Coletta, <u>Bryan</u>, pp. 311-44; Lansing, <u>War Memoirs</u>, pp. 43-53; Link, <u>Wilson: Campaigns for Progressivism and Peace</u>, pp. 605-17, and also <u>Wilson: Confusions and Crises, 1915-1917</u>. Princeton, N.J.: Princeton University Press, 1964, pp. 55-100; Charles Seymour, ed. <u>The Intimate Papers of Colonel House</u>, 4 vols. Boston: Houghton Mifflin, 1926-1928, 2:13-18.

11. CAPT Thomas G. Frothingham, USNR, <u>The Naval History of the World War</u>, 3 vols. Cambridge, Mass.: Harvard University Press, 1924-1926, 2:80-4.

12. Birnbaum, <u>Peace Moves and U-Boat Warfare</u>, pp. 32-38; Link, <u>Wilson: Confusion and Crises</u>, pp. 683-87, and <u>Wilson: Campaigns for Progressivism and Peace</u>, pp. 11-12, 120-35; Seymour, ed. <u>Papers of Colonel House</u>, 2:199-204.

13. Birnbaum, <u>Peace Moves and U-boat Warfare</u>, pp. 46-61; GEN Erich von Falkenhayn, <u>General Headquarters, 1914-1916, and Its Critical Decisions</u>. London: Hutchinson, 1919.

14. Birnbaum, <u>Peace Moves and U-boat Warfare</u>, pp. 46-61; Link, <u>Wilson: Confusion and Crises</u>, pp. 11-12, 120-35, and <u>Wilson: Campaigns for Progressivism and Peace</u>, pp. 239-51; Falkenhayn, <u>General Headquarters</u>, pp. 239-51; Michelsen, <u>Submarine Warfare, 1914-1917</u>, pp. 30-4.

15. Corbett and Newbolt, <u>Naval Operations</u>, 2:280-7;

Falkenhayn, <u>General Headquarters</u>, pp. 220-3, 252-54; Frothingham, <u>Naval History of the World War</u>, 2:118-25, 133-34; Gibson and Prendergast, <u>German Submarine War</u>, pp. 81-82, 88-89; Scheer, <u>Germany's High Sea Fleet</u>, pp. 105, 234-37; Tirpitz, <u>Memoirs</u>, 2:171-72.

CHAPTER 4

1. ADM Scheer, <u>Germany's High Sea Fleet in the World War</u>. New York: Peter Smith, 1934, pp. 113-22.

2. Julian Corbett and Henry Newbolt, <u>History of the Great War, Based on Official Documents: Naval Operations</u>, 5 vols. London: Longmans, Green, 1920-1931, 2:289-309; Georg von Hase, <u>Kiel and Jutland</u>. London: Skeffington, 1921, pp. 67-69; John Rushworth Jellicoe, <u>The Grand Fleet 1914-1916: Its Creation, Development and Work</u>. New York: George H. Doran, 1919, pp. 275-79; A. Temple Patterson, <u>Tyrwhitt of the Harwich Force: The Life of Admiral of the Fleet Sir Reginald Tyrwhitt</u>. London: Macdonald, 1973, pp. 156-59.

3. Scheer, <u>Germany's High Sea Fleet</u>, pp. 133-35.

4. Corbett and Newbolt, <u>Naval Operations</u>, 2:322-25; Langhorne Gibson and J.E.T. Harper, <u>The Riddle Jutland: An Authentic History</u>. New York: Coward-McCann, 1934, pp. 99-100; Jellicoe, <u>Grand Fleet</u>, p. 316; Scheer, <u>Germany's High Sea Fleet</u>, pp. 135-40.

5. Corbett and Newbolt, <u>Naval Operations</u>, 2:326a-29; Gibson and Harper, <u>Riddle of Jutland</u>, pp. 107-11, 129-39; Jellicoe, <u>Grand Fleet</u>, pp. 208-21; Arthur J. Marder, <u>From the Dreadnought to Scapa Flow: The Royal Navy in the Fisher Era, 1904-1919</u>, 5 vols. London: Oxford University Press. Vol. 3 <u>Jutland and After (May 1916-December 1916)</u>, pp. 37-61; Scheer, <u>Germany's High Sea Fleet</u>, pp. 135-40.

6. Reginald H. Bacon, <u>The Jutland Scandal</u>, 4th ed. London: Hutchinson, 1925, p. 67; RADM. William S. Chalmers, RN, <u>The Life and Letters of David Beatty, Admiral of the Fleet</u>. London: Hodder

and Stoughton, 1951, p. 243; Gibson and Harper, Riddle of Jutland, pp. 164-65; Jellicoe, Grand Fleet, pp. 326, 331-32; Marder, Jutland, p. 81; Scheer, Germany's High Sea Fleet, pp. 150-1.

7. In his account, The Jutland Scandal, ADM Bacon was hard on Beatty, saying that "Again on the run North not one signal was conveying information to the Commander-in-Chief; and lastly, Admiral Beatty completely lost touch with the High Sea Battlefleet, so that he joined the Grand Fleet battlefleet, dumb and unable to supply the Commander-in-Chief with the information which was vital to him to determine the method of his deployment; and this in spite of his having no less that [thirteen light cruisers and the seaplane carrier Engadine] under his orders, one only of which if properly stationed, would have kept him supplied with the necessary information." Marder, Jutland, seconds Bacon.

8. Hurd cited in Gibson and Harper, Riddle of Jutland, p. ix.

9. Winston Churchill, The World Crisis, 4 vols, in 1. New York: Charles Scribner's Sons, 1931, pp. 640-1; Hase, Kiel and Jutland, pp. 183-89; Jellicoe, Grand Fleet, pp. 345-48; Marder, Jutland, pp. 86-105. According to Carlyon Bellairs, The Battle of Jutland: The Sowing and the Reaping. London: Hodder and Stoughton, 1920, p. 35, "The practice of turning away from enemy destroyers of course meant to turn away from the enemy battleships and victory. The turn away was the defensive measure which lost us the victory at Jutland. . . ." A similar conclusion is reached by Capt. Wayne Hughes, USN (Ret.), Fleet Tactics: Theory and Practice. Annapolis, Md.: Naval Institute Press, 1986, pp. 79-83.

10. Corbett and Newbolt, Naval Operations, 2:371.

11. See for example, Cyril Falls, The Great War. New York: Capricorn Books, 1959, p. 214; and Marder, Jutland, pp. 115-22.

12. Bacon, Jutland Scandal, pp. 81-83; Corbett and Newbolt, Naval Operations, 2:375-83; Gibson and Harper, Riddle of Jutland, pp. 194-203; Scheer, Germany's High Sea Fleet, pp. 155-58.

13. Donald Macintyre, <u>Jutland</u>. London: Evans Bros., 1937, p. 140. The sentiment is repeated in CAPT Joseph M. Reeves, USN, "The Battle of Jutland." Typescript of lecture delivered at the Army War College, Washington DC., 1925.

14. Hase cited in Bacon, <u>Jutland Scandal</u>, p. 85.

15. Great Britain, Admiralty. <u>Battle of Jutland: Official Despatches</u>. London: HMSO, 1920; Jellicoe, <u>Grand Fleet</u>, pp. 370-3.

16. Bacon, <u>Jutland Scandal</u>, pp. 92-95, and Appendix A; Corbett and Newbolt, <u>Naval Operations</u>, 2:395-98; Hase, <u>Kiel and Jutland</u>, pp. 218-22; Jellicoe, <u>Grand Fleet</u>, pp. 381-84; Marder, <u>Jutland</u>, pp. 140-62; Scheer, <u>Germany's High Sea Fleet</u>, p. 172. While avoiding strategic considerations, John Campbell, <u>Jutland: An Analysis of the Fighting</u>. Annapolis, Md.: Naval Institute Press, 1986, meticulously notes the damage done to all ships by every gun that was fired on both sides.

17. Corbett and Newbolt, <u>Naval Operations</u>, 2:416-18; Gibson and Harper, <u>Riddle of Jutland</u>, pp. 231-33; Hase, <u>Kiel and Jutland</u>, pp. 218-22; CDR John Irving, RN, Ret., <u>The Smoke Screen of Jutland</u>. New York: David McKay, 1967, pp. 242-43; Jellicoe, <u>Grand Fleet</u>, pp. 381-86; Marder, <u>Jutland</u>, pp. 140-62; Scheer, <u>Germany's High Sea Fleet</u>, p. 162.

18. Hugo Waldeyer-Hartz, <u>Admiral von Hipper</u>. Trans. by F. Appleby Holt. London: Rich & Cowan, 1933, p. 221.

19. Churchill, <u>World Crisis</u>, p. 612. For additional claims and counterclaims of victory at Jutland, see Bellairs, <u>Battle of Jutland</u>, pp. 261-67; Geoffrey Bennett, <u>The Battle of Jutland</u>. London: Batsford, 1964, pp. 55-77; Gibson and Harper, <u>Riddle of Jutland</u>, pp. 253-94; Charles C. Gill, <u>What Happened at Jutland</u>. New York: George H. Doran, 1921, pp. 165-70; Macintyre, <u>Jutland</u>, pp. 186-94; Marder, <u>Jutland</u>, pp. 165-212; and Henry Newbolt, <u>A Naval History of the War</u>. London: Hodder and Stoughton, 1920, pp. 313-40.

20. K.G.B. Dewar, <u>The Navy from Within</u>. London:

Victor Gollancz, 1939, pp. 270-1, 274, 280;
ADM Sir Frederick C. Dreyer, The Sea Heritage.
London: Museum Press, 1955, pp. 83-85. See also
CAPT E. Altham, RN, Jellicoe. London: Blackie,
1938, pp. 115-66, and Bennett, Battle of Jutland, with the latter saying that Jellicoe
"could never delegate and rest happy in his
mind."

21. Jellicoe, Grand Fleet, pp. 397-98.

22. Amiral [Raoul V.P.] Castex, Theories Strategi-
     ques, Vol. 2, Ch. 6. The German Operations in
     the North Sea (1914-1916). Trans. by LCDR
     Charles Moran, USNR. Stenciled and printed at
     the Naval War College, Newport, Rhode Island,
     Sept. 1932, p. 63.

23. Falls, Great War, p. 216.

24. Otto Groos, Der Krieg Zur See, 1914-1918. The
     North Sea: War at Sea, 1914-1918. Vol. 5,
     Chaps. 1, 2, and 3 trans. by Joseph A. Wise and
     William E. Bauer. Newport, Rhode Island: Naval
     War College, 1935, 5:446; Irving, Smoke Screen
     of Jutland, p. 7; "Statement of the Chief of
     the Admiralty Staff of the Navy on the Battle of
     Jutland." In Ralph H. Lutz, ed. The Fall of the
     German Empire, 1914-1918, 2 vols. Stanford:
     Stanford University Press, 1932, 1:671-73.

25. C. Ernest Fayle, Seaborne Trade: History of the
     Great War Based on Official Documents, 3 vols.
     New York: Longmans, Green, 1920-1933, 2:275-312,
     3:36-39, 90-1; Louis Guichard, The Naval Block-
     ade, 1914-1918. New York: D. Appleton and Co.,
     1930, pp. 834-87; David Lloyd George, War Mem-
     oirs of David Lloyd George, 6 vols. Boston:
     Little, Brown, 1933-1937, 3:43-44.

26. Corbett and Newbolt, Naval Operations, 4:337;
     Richard H. Gibson and Maurice Prendergast, The
     German Submarine War, 1914-1918. New York:
     Richard R. Smith, 1931, pp. 112-15; Guichard,
     The Naval Blockade, 1914-1918, pp. 93-95; 101-
     6; Albert Gayer, "Summary of German Submarine
     Operations in the Various Theaters of War from
     1914 to 1918," USNIP 52 (Apr. 1926):625.

27. Corbett and Newbolt, Naval Operations, 5:3-14;
     Lloyd George, Memoirs, 3:79-90-; RADM William

Sowden Sims, U.S. Navy, in collaboration with Burton J. Hendrick, <u>The Victory at Sea</u>. New York: Doubleday, Page and Co., 1920, pp. 103-5.

28. Harford M. Hyde, <u>Carson: The Life of Sir Edward Carson</u>. London: Heinemann, 1953, pp. 413-18; Lloyd George, <u>Memoirs</u>, 3:90.

29. Sir Frederick B. Maurice, <u>Lessons of Allied Co-operation: Naval, Military, and Air, 1914-1918</u>. New York: Oxford University Press, 1942, pp. 20, 26, 73-74; B.H. Liddell Hart, <u>The Real War 1914-1918</u>. London: Faber and Faber, 1930, pp. 199-200; Charles A Court Repington, <u>The First World War, 1914-1918</u>, 2 vols. Boston: Houghton Mifflin, 1920, 1:371-74, 383-84, 391-92; Lloyd George, <u>Memoirs</u>, 4:329-69.

30. Lord Hankey, <u>The Supreme Command</u>, 2 vols. London: George Allen & Unwin, 1961, 2:610-11; Lloyd George, <u>Memoirs</u>, 4:322-50; Maurice, <u>Lessons of Allied Cooperation</u>, pp. 74-75.

31. C.R.M.F. Cruttwell, <u>A History of the Great War 1914-1918</u>, 2d ed. Oxford: Clarendon Press, 1936, pp. 436-42; Hankey, <u>Supreme Command</u>, 2:5610-31; Maurice, <u>Lessons of Allied Cooperation</u>, pp. 80-96.

32. Air Chief Marshal Sir Arthur Longmore, <u>From Sea to Sky 1910-1915</u>. London: Geoffrey Bles, 1946, pp. 69-70; Arthur J. Marder, <u>From the Dreadnought to Scapa Flow: The Royal Navy in the Fisher Era, 1904-1919</u>, 5 vols. London: Oxford University Press, 1961-1966. Vol. 4. <u>1917: Year of Crisis</u>, pp. 21-24.

33. "The Peace Proposal, December 12, 1916." In Lutz, ed. <u>Fall of the German Empire</u>, 1:398-99, and "Reply of the Imperial Government to President Wilson, December 26, 1916," ibid., 1:399-400; Cruttwell, <u>History of the Great War</u>, pp. 360-5; Hankey, <u>Supreme Command</u>, 2:602-3; Sterling J. Kernak, <u>Distractions of Peace During War: The Lloyd George Government's Reactions to Woodrow Wilson December 1916-November 1918</u>. Philadelphia: Transactions of the American Philosophical Society, NS 65, pt. 2, 1975.

34. Scheer, <u>Germany's High Sea Fleet</u>, pp. 188-90.

35. Karl E. Birnbaum, <u>Peace Moves and U-boat War-</u>

fare: A Study of Imperial Germany's Policy Toward the United States, April 18, 1916-January
9, 1917. Stockholm: Almquist & Wiksell, 1958,
pp. 27-327; Corbett and Newbolt, Naval Operations, 4:229-75; Statements in Germany, Nation-
alversammlung, 1919-1920. Trans. Official German Documents Relating to the World War, 2 vols.
New York: Oxford University Press, 1923, 1:
483-85, 501; Scheer, Germany's High Sea Fleet,
pp. 190-1, 343-63; Karl Tschuppik, Ludendorff:
The Tragedy of a Military Mind. Trans. W.H.
Johnson. New York: Houghton Mifflin, 1932, pp.
82-84.

36. Alice M. Morrissey, "The United States and the
     Rights of Neutrals, 1917-1918," American Jour-
     nal of International Law 31 (Jan. 1937):24.

37. Fayle, Seaborne Trade, 3:39; Lloyd George, Mem-
     oirs, 3:75.

38. Bradley A. Fiske, Diary, MDLC, entry of Sept.
     29, 1914.

39. U.S. Congress. House Committee on Naval Af-
     fairs. Hearings before the Committee on Naval
     Affairs, the House of Representatives, on Esti-
     ates Submitted by the Secretary of the Navy,
     1915. Washington: GPO, 1915, pp. 34-37, 282,
     288.

40. GB to SECNAV, 17 Nov. 1914, GB Records, No.
     420-2. Washington: Naval Historical Center,
     Operational Archives; Josephus Daniels, Diary,
     Jan. 5, 22, 24, 25, 1915, Josephus Daniels
     Papers, MDLC; Paolo E. Coletta, Bradley A.
     Fiske and the American Navy. Lawrence; Regents
     Press of Kansas, 1979, pp. 131-48.

41. GB to SECNAV, Jan. 28, 1915, GB-425, GB Records;
     Coletta, Fiske, pp. 142-59.

42. New York Times, Dec. 25, 1915; Daniels, Diary,
     Feb. 27, Mar. 6, 8, 9, 10, 12, 13, 19, 20, 29,
     Apr. 2,7, 1917; Annual Report of the Secretary
     of the Navy, 1916. Washington: GPO, 1916, pp.
     4-5, 11, 75-76; Arthur S. Link, Wilson: Confu-
     sions and Crises, 1916-1917. Princeton, N.J.:
     Princeton University Press, 1965, pp. 588-93,
     and Wilson: The Struggle for Neutrality, 1914-
     1915. Princeton, N.J.: Princeton University

Press, 1960, pp. 15, 35-36.

43. Senior Member Present, GB, to SECNAV, 24 Mar. 1917, GB 425, Conf. Senior Member Present, GB, to SECNAV, 5 Apr. 1917, GB No. 425; Coletta, Fiske, pp. 187-92.

44. Sims to Mrs. Sims, 10 Feb. 1917, William S. Sims Papers, MDLC; Daniels, Diary, Feb. 25, 27, Mar. 8, 25, 1917; Coletta, Fiske, pp. 184-85; Elting E. Morison, Admiral Sims and the Modern American Navy. Boston: Houghton Mifflin, 1942, p. 337; Charles Seymour, ed., The Intimate Papers of Colonel House, 4 vols. Boston: Houghton Mifflin, 1926-1928, 2:454-60; Sims and Hendrick, Victory at Sea, pp. 3-4. Other events that stimulated Wilson to go to war were the Russian Revolution of March 1917, which he read to mean that Russia would henceforth be a democracy, and the Zimmermann Note. In the latter, the German foreign secretary wrote to the German minister in Mexico on Jan. 16, 1917, that in the event of war with the United States an attempt should be made to obtain an alliance with Mexico in return to Mexico's regaining the territory she had lost to the United States in 1848. See Barbara Tuchman, The Zimmermann Telegram. New York: Viking, 1958.

CHAPTER 5

1. Josephus Daniels, Diary, Apr. 7, 9, 11, 12, 1917, Josephus Daniels Papers, MDLC; Conf. Senior Member Present, GB to SECNAV, 5 Apr. 1917, GB No. 425, Serial 699, and GB Studies, 425, Serials 688, 689, 696, and 700. Washington: Naval Historical Center, Operational Archives.

2. Daniels, Diary, Apr. 22, May 5, 22, 1917; Josephus Daniels, The Wilson Era: Years of War, 1917-1923. Chapel Hill: University of North Carolina Press, 1946, p. 48; David Lloyd George, War Memoirs of David Lloyd George, 6 vols. Boston: Little, Brown, 1933-1937, 3:540-44; W.G. Lyddon, British War Missions to the United States, 1914-1918. New York: Oxford University Press, 1938, pp. viii, 17-39; Arthur Willert, The Road to Safety: A Study of Anglo-American Relations. New York; Praeger, 1953, pp. 73-80.

3. Daniel, Diary, Aug. 4, 1917; Louis Guichard, The Naval Blockade 1914-1918. New York: D. Appleton, 1930, pp. 100-4; Mary Klachko, "Anglo-American Naval Competition, 1918-1922." Ph.D. diss., Columbia University, 1962, 9 n3.

4. Archibald Low, Mine and Countermine. London: Hutchinson, 1940, p. 86; ADM of the Fleet Jellicoe, The Submarine Peril: The Admiralty Policy in 1917. London: Cassell, 1934, pp. 1-18, 35-37; The Jellicoe-Sims conversation is reported in RADM William Sowden Sims, U.S. Navy, in collaboration with Burton J. Hendrick, The Victory at Sea. New York: Doubleday, Page, 1920, pp. 9-11.

5. Sims to Mrs. Sims, 19 Apr. 1917, William S. Sims Papers, MDLC; Burton J. Hendrick The Life and Letters of Walter H. Page, 3 vols. Garden City, N.Y.: Doubleday, Page, 1924-1926, 2:2780; Jellicoe, Submarine Peril, pp. 70-1; Elting E. Morison, Admiral William S. Sims and the Modern American Navy. Boston: Houghton Mifflin, 1942, pp. 345-53; Sims and Hendrick, Victory at Sea, pp. 45, 47, 374-76. Several U-boats operated in northern American and Canadian Atlantic waters during the summer of 1918. They did some damage but failed to stop American concentration on A/S operations in British waters. Among many other accounts see William Bell Clark, When the U-Boats Came to America. Boston: Little, Brown, 1929, and Henry Johnson James, German Subs in Yankee Waters: First World War. New York: Gotham House, 1940.

6. Sims to Daniels, 18 apr. 1917, Sims to William S. Benson, 19 Apr. 1917, Sims Papers; Jellicoe, Submarine Peril, p. 96.

7. Sims to Mrs. Sims, 22, 29 Apr. 1917, Sims Papers.

8. Sims to Mrs. Sims, 26, 29, 30 Apr. 1916, Sims Papers; Lloyd George, Memoirs, 3:106-8.

9. Sims to Daniels, 21, 22 June 1917, Sims Papers; Lloyd George, Memoirs, 3:112-22; Sims and Hendrick, Victory at Sea, pp. 99-105, 113-17.

10. ADM Sir Lewis Bayly, Pull Together: The Memoirs

of <u>Admiral Sir Lewis Bayly</u>. London: George G. Harrap, 1939, pp. 227-28.

11. Pratt to Sims, 6 May, and n.d., but early Aug. 1917, Sims Papers; SECNAV to Sims, 10 July 1917, NARG 45, Box 580; Gerald E. Wheeler, <u>Admiral William Veazie Pratt, U.S. Navy: A Sailor's Life</u>. Washington: Naval History Division, 1974, pp. 92-95.

12. Bayly, <u>Pull Together</u>, pp. 219, 222; Sims and Hendrick, <u>Victory at Sea</u>, pp. 11-17.

13. Sims to Benson, 11 apr. 1917, Sims to Mrs. Sims, 31 May 1917, Sims Papers.

14. In condensed form, the policies stated that the United States would fully cooperate with the Allies in meeting the submarine threat against Allied sea lines of communication "subject only to maintaining an adequate defensive in home waters." However, "the future position of the United States must not in any way be jeopardized by an disintegration of our main fighting fleet." Last, the Navy Department stood ready "to discuss more fully any plans for joint operations with the Allies." Wilson to Sims, 5 July 1917, Sims Papers.

15. Daniels, Diary, 25 June, 23, 26 Nov. 1917, 31 Jan. 1918; Benson to Sims, 9 Jan. 1918, Sims to Benson, 31 Dec. 1917, 4, 10, 31 Jan., 21 Apr. 1918, Sims to Mrs. Sims 6, 8, 9 June 1917, 8, 24 Jan. 1918, Sims to Wilson, 7 July 1917, Sims Papers.

16. Sims to Mrs. Sims, 26 July, 9 Aug., 24, 27 Sept., 1, 14 Oct. 1917, Sims Papers; Daniels, Diary, 24, 27 July, 11, 13, 18 Aug. 1917; Dean C. Allard, "Anglo-American Naval Differences During World War I," MA 44 (Oct. 1980):78.

17. Sims to Mrs. Sims, 18, 20 July 1917, Sims Papers; Lord Hankey, <u>The Supreme Command</u>, 2 vols. London: George Allen & Unwin, 1961, 2:629-53; Jellicoe, <u>Crisis of the Naval War</u>, pp. 164-75, and <u>Submarine Peril</u>, pp. 71-81; Julian S. Corbett and Henry Newbolt, <u>History of the Great War, Based on Official Documents</u>, 5 vols. London: Longmans, Green, 1920-1931, 5:120-23 (after Corbett died, Newbolt wrote vol.

5, and so will be cited hereafter); Arthur
J. Arthur J. Marder, <u>From the Dreadnought
to Scapa Flow: The Royal Navy in the Fisher Era,
1904-1919</u>.
5 vols. London: Oxford University Press, 1961-
1966. Vol. 4. <u>1917: Year of Crisis</u>, pp. 167-81;
COMMO G. von Schoultz, <u>With the British Battle
Fleet: Recollections of a Russian Naval Officer</u>.
Trans. by Arthur Chambers. London: Hutchinson,
1925, pp. 283-96 (Schoultz was the keenly per-
ceptive liaison officer with the Grand Fleet];
Sims and Hendrick, <u>Victory at Sea</u>, pp. 116, 163.

18.   Lloyd George to Wilson, 3 Sept. 1917, Woodrow
Wilson Papers, MDLC. The letter is printed in
Lloyd George, <u>Memoirs</u>, 4:518-24.

19.   Daniels, Diary, 11, 12, 27, 28 Oct. 1917: Lloyd
George, <u>Memoirs</u>, 5:30001-2.

20.   David F. Trask, <u>The United States in the Supreme War Council: American War Aims and Inter-
Allied Strategy, 1917-1918</u>. Middletown, Conn.:
Weslyan University Press, 1961, pp. 20-38, 175,
181; U.S. Navy Department. ONI. Historical Section. Pub. No. 7. <u>The American Naval Planning
Section in London</u>. Washington: GPO, 1923, pp.
489-92.

21.   Sims to Mrs. Sims, 15, 19 Nov., 4 Dec. 1917,
Sims Papers.

22.   Daniels, Diary, 20 Dec. 1917.

23.   Sir Frederick Maurice, <u>Lessons of Allied Cooperation: Naval, Military, and Air, 1914-1918</u>.
New York: Oxford University Press, 1942, pp.
93-104.

24.   Daniels, Diary, 5, 6, Dec. 1917; Sims to Mrs.
Sims, 29 Dec. 1917, 14 Jan. 1918, Sims Papers;
Lloyd George, <u>Memoirs</u>, 3:134-35.

CHAPTER 6

1.   American naval efforts are described in part in
U.S. Navy Department. ONI. Historical Section.
Pub. No. 7. <u>The American Naval Planning Section
in London</u>. Washington: GPO, 1923. For the con-

tributions of U.S. naval air power, see Archibald Turnbull and Clifford Lord, <u>History of United States Naval Aviation</u>. New Haven: Yale University Press, 1949, pp. 124-41, and Adrian O. Van Wyen, <u>Naval Aviation in World War I</u>. Washington: GPO, 1969.

2. Paolo E. Coletta, "The Perils of Invention: Bradley A. Fiske and the Torpedo Plane," <u>American Neptune</u> 37 (June 1977):111-27.

3. Benedict Crowell and Robert F. Wilson, <u>How America Went to War. The Road to France: The Transportation of Troops and Military Supplies, 1917-1918</u>, 2 vols. New Haven: Yale University Press, 1921; Edward N. Hurley, <u>The Bridge to France</u>. Philadelphia: J.B. Lippincott, 1927; Peyton C. March, Gen, USA, <u>The Nation at War</u>. Garden City, N.Y.: Doubleday, Doran, 1932; Dorrell H. Smith and Paul U. Betters, <u>The United States Shipping Board</u>. Washington: Brookings Institution, 1931; J. Russell Smith, "Building Ships to Beat the U-boat," <u>American Review of Reviews</u> 56 (Oct. 1917):393-96; J.A. Furer, CDR USN, "The 110-Foot Submarine Chasers and Eagle Boats," USNIP 45 (May 1919):743-52.

4. RADM Ralph Earle, ed. <u>Naval Ordnance Activities: World War 1917-1918</u>. Washington: GPO, 1920.

5. VADM Albert Gleaves, USN, <u>A History of the Transport Service: Adventures and Experiences of United States Transports and Cruisers in World War I</u>. New York: George H. Doran, 1921.

6. Lewis P. Clephane, <u>History of the Naval Overseas Transportation Service in World War I</u>. Washington: Naval History Division, 1969.

7. Josephus Daniels, Diary, 29 Oct. 1917, Josephus Daniels Papers, MDLC, and <u>The Wilson Era: Years of War, 1917-1923</u>. Chapel Hill: University of North Carolina Press, 1946, p. 91.

8. Ralph Earle to Sims 11 June 1917, Woodrow Wilson to Sims, 4 July 1917, William S. Sims Papers, MDLC; data in Simon P. Fullinwider Papers, Washington: Museum of History and Technology; Earle, ed. <u>Naval Ordnance Activities: World War</u>, pp. 108-10; RADM William Sowden Sims, U.S. Navy, in collaboration with Burton J.

Hendrick, <u>The Victory at Sea</u>. Garden City, N.Y.: Doubleday, Page, 1920, pp. 286-91.

9. The mines comprised two steel hemispheres 34 inches in diameter that were welded together. The anchor, which weighed 816 pounds, included cable mooring lines. See Reginald R. Belknap, <u>The Yankee Mining Squadron</u>. Annapolis, Md.: U.S. Naval Institute, 1920; J.S. Cowie, CAPT RN, <u>Mines, Minelayers and Minelaying</u>. London: Oxford University Press, 1949; Robert C. Duncan, <u>America's Use of Sea Mines</u>. White Oak, Md.: U.S. Naval Ordnance Laboratory, Jan. 1962; John A. Roebling Co., <u>Wire Roping the German Submarine: The Barrage that Stopped the U-boat</u>. Trenton, N.J.: John A. Roebling Co., 1920.

10. Daniels, <u>Wilson Era: Years of War</u>, p. 91; Sims and Hendrick, <u>Victory at Sea</u>, p. 306.

11. Robert M. Grant, <u>U-Boat Intelligence 1914-1918</u>. Hamden, Conn.: Archon Books, 1969, p. 169, and <u>U-boats Destroyed: The Effect of Antisubmarine Warfare 1914-1918</u>. London: Putnam, 1964; Arthur J. Marder, <u>From the Dreadnought to Scapa Flow: The Royal Navy in the Fisher Era, 1904-1919</u>, 5 vols. New York: Oxford University Press, 1961-1966. Vol. 5. <u>Victory and Aftermath, January 1918-June 1919</u>, pp. 73-75.

12. Roger Keyes, <u>The Naval Memoirs of Admiral of Admiral of the Fleet Roger Keyes</u>, 2 vols. New York: E.P. Dutton, 1934-1935, 2:114-15.

13. Sims to Benson, 10 Jan. 1918; Niblack to Sims, 19 Jan. 1918, Sims Papers.

14. Bristol to Sims, 29 Dec. 1917, ibid.

15. Daniels, Diary, 19 Aug. 1918.

16. Marder, <u>Victory and Aftermath</u>, pp. 131-38.

17. David Lloyd George, <u>The War Memoirs of David Lloyd George</u>, 6 vols. Boston: Little, Brown, 1933-1937, 6:389, 446; Harvey A. DeWeerd, <u>President Wilson Fights His War: World War I and the American Intervention</u>. New York: Macmillan, 1968, p. 300; Richard O'Connor, <u>Black Jack Pershing</u>. Garden City, N.Y.: Doubleday, 1961, p. 213.

18.   Sims to Mrs. Sims, 24 Jan. 10, 18, 25 Feb., 8, 10 Mar. 1918, Sims Papers.

19.   Sims to Mrs. Sims, 16 Mar., 18 May 1918, ibid.

CHAPTER 7

1.   Joel Pringle to Sims, 11 June 1918, Sims to Pringle, 14 June 1918, William S. Sims Papers; MDLC; Thomas A. Bailey, The Policy of the United States toward the Neutrals, 1917-1918. Baltimore: Johns Hopkins Press, 1942, pp. 64-379; C. Ernest Fayle, Seaborne Trade: History of the Great War Based on Official Documents, 3 vols. London: Longmans, Green, 1920-1933, 3:363-70; Louis Guichard, The Naval Blockade 1914-1918. New York: D. Appleton, 1930, pp. 133-304.   See the tables of British, Allied, and neutral merchant ship losses for 1918 in Arthur J. Marder, From the Dreadnought to Scapa Flow: The Royal Navy in the Fisher Era, 1904-1919, 5 vols. London: Oxford University Press, 1961-1966. Vol. 5. Victory and Aftermath, January 1918-June 1919, pp. 78-79. 110-17, and tables of U-boat losses, pp. 118-20.

2.   Harvey DeWeerd, President Wilson Fights His War: World War I and the American Intervention. New York: Macmillan, 1968, p. 301.   See also Elting E. Morison, Admiral Sims and the Modern American Navy. Boston: Houghton Mifflin, 1942, pp. 419-23; RADM William Sowden Sims, U.S. Navy, and Burton J. Hendrick, The Victory at Sea. Garden City, N.Y.: Doubleday, Page, 1920, Ch. 3.

13.   Lord Hankey, The Supreme Command, 2 vols. London: George Allen & Unwin, 1961, 1:742-44.

4.   Ferdinand Foch, The Memoirs of Marshal Foch. Trans. by Col. T. Bentley Mott.   Garden City, N.Y.: Doubleday, Doran, 1931, pp. 478-64, 274-79; GEN Tasker H. Bliss, "The Unified Command," Foreign Affairs 1 (Dec. 1922):28-29.

5.   Daniels, Diary, 30 Mar. 1918, Josephus Daniels Papers, MDLC; Robert D. Heinl, Soldiers of the Sea: The United States Marine Corps, 1775-1962. Annapolis, Md.: U.S. Naval Institute, 1962, pp. 193-95; MGEN John A. Lejeune, U.S. Marine Corps,

The _Reminiscences of a Marine_. Philadelphia: Dorrance and Co., 1930, pp. 233-403.

6.   Julian S. Corbett and Henry Newbolt, _History of the Great War, Based on Official Documents: Naval Operations_, 5 vols. London: London: Longmans, Green, 1920-1931, 5:217-27; Richard Gibson and Maurice Prendergast, _The German Submarine War 1914-1918_. New York: Richard R. Smith, 1931, pp. 286-88.

7.   Holger H. Herwig, _"Luxury Fleet": The Imperial German Navy, 1888-1918_. London: George Allen & Unwin, 1980, pp. 240-41; Marder, _Victory and Aftermath_, pp. 143-56; Newbolt, _Naval Operations_, 5:230-40.

8.   LCOL C.A Court Repington, _The First World War, 1914-1918: Personal Experiences of Lieut.-Col. C.A Court Repington_, 2 vols. Boston: Houghton Mifflin, 1920, 2:286-92, 307. Among others, see CAPT A.F.B. Carpenter, _The Blocking of Zeebrugge_. London: Herbert Jenkins, 1922; Roger Keyes, _The Naval Memoirs of Admiral of the Fleet Sir Roger Keyes_, 2 vols. New York: E.P. Dutton, 1934-1935, 2:127-34; Newbolt, _Naval Operations_, 5:241-76; "The Attack on Zeebrugge and Ostend," Naval War Notes, USNIP 44 (June 1918):1377-78.

9.   Sims to Benson, 2 Apr., 17 May, 14 June 1918, Sims to Mrs. Sims, 10, 21 Apr., 13 June, 15 Aug. 1918, Pershing to Sims, 13 June 1918, Sims Papers.

10. Joint Note No. 37, quoted in Peyton C. March, GEN USA, _The Nation at War_. Garden City, N.Y.: Doubleday Doran, 1932, p. 157.

11. Wing Commander Hubert R Allen, _The Legacy of Lord Trenchard_. London: Collins, 1962; Fayle, _Seaborne Trade_, 3:400-06; Raymond H. Fredette, _The Sky on Fire: The First Battle of Britain_. New York: Holt, Rinehart & Winston, 1966; Paul Guinn, _British Strategy and Politics, 1914-1918_. Oxford: Clarendon Press, 1961, pp. 315-20.

12. ADM Scheer, _Germany's High Sea Fleet_. New York: Peter Smith, 1934, pp. 324-45; Alfred von Tirpitz, _My Memoirs_, 2 vols. New York: Dodd, Mead, 1919, 2:117.

13. U.S. Navy Department. ONI, Historical Section, Pub. No. 7. <u>The American Naval Planning Section in London</u>. Washington: GPO, 1923, pp. 417-19; Foch, <u>Memoirs</u>, pp. 451-52; Harry R. Rudin, <u>Armistice 1918</u>. New Haven: Yale University Press, 1944, pp. 12-61, 93-97.

14. Rudin, <u>Armistice 1918</u>, pp. 98-99.

15. Ibid., pp. 93-94; Newbolt, <u>Naval Operations</u>, 5:364

16. Hankey, <u>Supreme Command</u>, 2:853-55; David F. Trask, <u>Captains & Cabinets: Anglo-American Naval Relations, 1917-1918</u>. Columbia: University of Missouri Press, 1972, pp. 318-24; Lady Wester Wemyss, <u>The Life and Letters of Lord Wester Wemyss, Admiral of the Fleet</u>. London: Eyre and Spottiswoode, 1935, pp. 385-87.

17. "Conference at the Office of the Imperial Chancellor (Extract)." In Ralph H. Lutz, ed., <u>Fall of the German Government, 1914-1918</u>, 2 vols. Stanford: Stanford University Press, 1932, 2: 466-70; "The Reply of October 12, 1918, to President Wilson's Note of October 8, 1918," ibid., 2:471-72; "Full Session of October 17, 1918," ibid., 2:472-95; and "The Third German Note, October 20, 1918," ibid., 2:495-96.

18. Daniels Diary, 3 Nov. 1918; Trask, <u>Captains & Cabinets</u>, pp. 219-31.

19. Allied Naval Council, Sixth Meeting: Paris and Versailles. Paper No. 260, dated 5 Dec. 1918. See herein No. 2. Conference of Naval Representatives, 28 October 1918, Paris; Appendix A. Naval Conditions of Armistice with Germany and Austria-Hungary Proposed by Great Britain and France; Appendix C. Complete Draft of Naval Conditions for the Armistice with Germany; Appendix D. Complete Draft of Naval Conditions for the Armistice with Austria-Hungary.

20. Edward M. House, Diary, 28 Oct. 1918, Edward M. House Papers, Sterling Memorial Library, Yale University; Sims to Mrs. Sims, 4 Nov. 1918, Sims Papers; Hankey, <u>Supreme Command</u>, 2:857-60; Rudin, <u>Armistice 1918</u>, pp. 402-5; Trask, <u>Captains & Cabinets</u>, pp. 336-41; Mary Klachko, "Anglo-American Naval Competition, 1918-1922."

Ph.D. diss., Columbia University, 1962, pp. 53-152.

21. American Naval Planning Section in London, pp. 457-60; Trask, Captains & Cabinets, pp. 343-47.

22. American Naval Planning Section in London, pp. 439-44. American naval thought and activity with respect to the naval terms of the Armistice and of the Treaty of Versailles may be followed in Planning Committee [of the Office of the Chief of Naval Operations] to the Chief of Naval Operations, 27 Nov. 1918; GB Memorandum for Chief of Naval Operations, 2 Dec. 1918, GB No. 438, Serial No. 897; and U.S. Navy Department, Division of Naval Intelligence, United States Naval Activity in Connection with the Armistice of 1918 and The Peace Conference of 1919, GB 429-2, 31 Mar. 1944.

23. RADM William Scott Chalmers, The Life and Letters of David Beatty, Admiral of the Fleet. London: Hodder and Stoughton, 1951, p.343.

24. Herwig, "Luxury Fleet," pp. 247-48; Marder, Victory and Aftermath, pp. 66-68; Scheer, Germany's High Sea Fleet, pp. 322-53.

25. Scheer, Germany's High Sea Fleet, pp. 353-56.

CHAPTER 8

1. Italy. Marina. Stato Maggiore. Ufficio Storico della Marina Militare. La Marina italiana nella grande guerra, 8 vols. Firenze: Vallechi Editore, 1935-1942, 1:156-78, 380-1 (hereafter cited as MI); Archibald Hurd, Italian Sea Power and the Great War. London: Constable & Co., 1918, pp. 17-24; Antonio Salandra, Italy and the Great War: From Neutrality to Intervention. Trans. by Zoe Kendrick Pyne. London: Edward Arnold, 1932, pp. 217-62.

2. Camillo Manfroni, I Nostri alleati navale: Ricordi della guerra Adriatica 1915-1918. Milano: A. Mondadori, 1927, pp. 21-22; MI, 1:303-4, 375-78.

3. MI, 1:211-37, 402-3; Salandra, Italy and the Great War, pp. 35, 46; Luigi Villari, The War

on the Italian Front. London: Cobden-Sanderson, 1932, p. 238.

4. MI, 1:253, 300; Anthony Sokol, **The Imperial and Royal Austro-Hungarian Navy**. Annapolis, Md.: U.S. Naval Institute, 1968, p. 94; Paul G. Halpern, The Naval War in the Mediterranean 1914-1918. Annapolis, Md.: Naval Institute Press, 1987. pp. 1-83. 125-70.

5. MI, 1:313-24, 359-68.
5. MI. ;"313-24. 359-68.

6. Ibid., 1:331-41; Sokol, Austro-Hungarian Navy, pp. 87-89.

7. MI, 1:331-41. Di Revel, born in 1859, was trained at several naval schools. As a lieutenant he gained an enviable reputation for skill in maneuvering destroyers. After three years in administrative posts ashore and a two-year tour in command of a battleship, he commanded a division of four cruisers during the Italo-Turkish War. On 1 April 1913 he was named the chief of the naval staff and in that billet prepared his navy for the Great War. From October 1915 he commanded the Department of Venice, after which he again became chief of the naval staff and in addition commander of the operating forces. G.V. (CM) Salvatore Specchio, Vice Chief of the Italian Naval History Office, to the writer, 21 April 1978.

8. Italia. Ufficio Storico della R. Marina. Impiego delle forze navale: operazioni, 18 vols. Vol. 3. Apertura delle ostilitá in mare; Lega Navale Italiana. La Marina Italiana nella Guerra Mondiale. Rome: La Lega, 1920, Diary, p. 3.

9. Nicholas Horthy, Memoirs. New York: Roger Speller & Sons, 1937, pp. 71-72; MI, 2:7-12, 67-70; Sokol, Austro-Hungarian Navy, pp. 107-9. See also Rene Greger, Austro-Hungarian Warships of World War I. London: Ian Allen, 1976.

10. Cyril Falls, The Great War 1914-1918. New York: Capricorn Books, 1959, pp. 23-26; B.H. Liddell Hart, The Real War 1914-1918. London: Faber & Faber, 1930, p. 136; MI, 2:96-105; MI, 2:216-67; Villari, War on the Italian Front, pp. 39-101; Amm di Squadra (c.a.) Giuseppe Fioravanzo,

"Cannoni navali alla fronte terrestra," Rivista Marittima 103 (Jan. 1970):35-55, and "I caccia-torpediniere dalle origini al 1922," Ibid. 96 (July-Aug. 1963):7-34.

11. MI, 2:116-27.

12. Ibid., 2:116-45; GEN Sq. A. Felice Porro, La Guerra nell'aria 1915-1918. Milano: Edizione Mate, 1935, pp. 29-52.

13. MI, 2:268-78.

14. Ibid., 2:283-300; Richard H. Gibson and Maurice Prendergast, The German Submarine War 1914-1918. New York: richard R. Smith, 1921, p. 124; Manfroni, I Nostri alleati navale, pp. 53-55; Auguste A. Thomazi, CAPT French Navy, La Guerre navale dans l'Adriatique. Paris; Payot, 1925, pp. 101-6.

15. MI, 2:308-14. Sokol, Austro-Hungarian Navy, pp. 115-16, says that a time bomb had been smuggled aboard by Italian traitors in Austrian pay.

16. Impiego delle forze navali: Operazioni. Vol. 5. Azione navale del 29 Dicembre 1915 nel Basso Adriatico; Manfroni, I Nostri alleati navale, pp. 61-63; MI, 2:439-66.

17. Hankey, Supreme Command, 2:484.

18. First Earl of Oxford and Asquith, Memoirs and Reflections, 2 vols. Boston: Little, Brown, 1928, 2:142-43.

19. K.G.B. Dewar, The Navy from Within. London: Victor Gollancz, 1939, pp. 202-3.

20. Manfroni, I Nostri alleati navale, pp. 111-25.

21. Erminio Bagnasco, I MAS e le Motosiluranti Italiane 1906-1968, 2d ed. Roma: Marina. Stato Maggiore. Ufficio Storico della Marina Italiana, 1969, pp. 611-13; Sokol, Austro-Hungarian Navy, pp. 122-23. Of the 422 MAS ordered, 244 were available for operations before the war ended.

22. MI, 3:56-63; Amm. Sq. Giuseppe Fioravanzo, "I treni armati della Marina," Rivista Marittima 99 (1966):13-26.

23. MI, 3:70-89.

24. Ibid., 3:114-16; Sokol, <u>Austro-Hungarian Navy</u>, p. 124.

25. Lega Navale, <u>La Marina Italiana nella Guerra Mondiale</u>, pp. 150-6; MI, 3:116-22; Sokol, <u>Austro-Hungarian Navy</u>, p. 124.

26. Great Britain. Office of the Chief of Staff of the Royal Navy (Historical Section). <u>Authentic History of the Italian-Austrian Naval War, 1915-1918</u>. Washington: Navy Department. ONI. Copy dated 1977 in NARG 45; Manfroni, <u>I Nostri alleati navale</u>, pp. 69-81, 91-110; VADM Henri Salaun, <u>La Marine Francaise</u>. Paris: Les Editions de France, 1934, pp. 211-25; Halpern, <u>Naval War in the Mediterranean</u>, pp. 228-306.

27. Julian S. Corbett and Henry Newbolt, <u>History of the Great War, Based on Official Documents: Naval Operations</u>, 5 vols. London: Longmans, Green, 1920-1931, 4:288-891; Gibson and Prendergast, <u>German Submarine War</u>, p. 127; Sokol, <u>Austro-Hungarian Navy</u>, p. 123.

28. MI, 3:322-26; Thomazi, <u>La Guerre navale dan l'Adriatique</u>, pp. 141-44.

29. MI, 4:19-29; Thomazi, <u>La Guerre navale dans l'Adriatique</u>, pp. 145-47; VADM C.V. Usborne, <u>Smoke on the Horizon: Mediterranean Fighting 1914-1918</u>. London: Hodder and Stoughton, 1933, pp. 262-67.

30. MI, 4:29-41, 45-79, 144-57.

31. Ibid., 4:256-57, 270-5; Salaun, <u>La Marine Francaise</u>, pp. 253-55.

32. Mark Kerr, <u>Land, Sea and Air: Reminiscences of Mark Kerr</u>. New York: Longmans, Green, 1927, pp. 205-12.

33. MI, 4:381-445.

34. Gibson and Prendergast, <u>German Submarine War</u>, pp. 253-55; Horthy, <u>Memoirs</u>, pp. 81-85; MI, 4:475-81; Sokol, <u>Austro-Hungarian Navy</u>, pp. 129-30; Thomazi, <u>La Guerre dans l'Adriatique</u>, pp. 147-52.

35. David Lloyd George, War Memoirs of David Lloyd George, 6 vols. Boston: Little, Brown, 1933-1937, 4:222-23, 234-51, 262-319; Edmund von Glaise Horstenau, The Collapse of the Austro-Hungarian Empire. Trans. by Ian F.D. Morrow. London: J.M. Dent, 1930, pp. 49-53; Arthur S. Link, Wilson: Campaigns for Progressivism and Peace 1916-1917. Princeton, N.J.: Princeton University Press, 1965, pp. 385-89.

36. Gibson and Prendergast, German Submarine War, pp. 256, 261-62; Manfroni, I Nostri alleati navale, pp. 45, 86-87, 187-92; MI, 6:48, 52-59, 76-82, 105-202, 309-12; Murray F. Sueter, Airmen or Noahs. . . . London: Sir I. Pitman, 1928, pp. 43-45.

37. MI, 6:27-52; Newbolt, Naval Operations, 5:82-83.

38. MGEN Sir George Aston, The Biography of the Late Marshal Foch. New York: Macmillan, 1929, pp. 184-85; Cyril Falls, The Battle of Caporetto. New York: J. B. Lippincott, 1966; Lloyd George, Memoirs, 4:468-81, 488; Newbolt, Naval Operations, 5:77 n1.

39. Paul Guinn, British Strategy and Politics, 1914-1918. Oxford: Clarendon Press, 1966; Lloyd George, Memoirs, 4:499-503; MI, 6:357-59.

40. Lloyd George, Memoirs, 6:385-92; MI, 6:392; Thomazi, La Guerre navale dans l'Adriatique, pp. 170-1.

41. MI, 6:431-44; Sokol, Austro-Hungarian Navy, p. 124; Usborne, Smoke on the Horizon, pp. 281-87; LCDR E.E. Hazlett, USN, "Davids of the Sea," USNIP 54 (Dec. 1928):1035-40.

42. Sir Walter Raleigh and Henry A. Jones, The War in the Air: Official History of the War, Based on Official Documents, 6 vols. Oxford: Clarendon Press, 1922-1934, 5:410-14; MI, 6:524-34, 7:233-35, 283.

43. Sims to SECNAV (Operations), Allied Naval Council Letters, NARG 45, QC; "Minutes of the ANC, First Session, Jan. 22, 1918," and "Third Session, Jan. 23, 1918," ibid; Sims to Benson, 15 Feb. 1918, William S. Sims Papers, MDLC; Halpern, Naval War in Mediterranean, pp. 357-

497; U.S. Navy Department. ONI. Historical Section. Pub. No. 7. The American Naval Planning Section in London. Washington: GPO, 1923, pp. 59-77, 137-38, 224, 248-49, 252-54; GEN Alberto Baldini, Diaz. Trans. W.J. Monson. London: Humphrey Toulmin, 1935, pp. 116-36; MI, 7:188-98, 200-2; Sokol, Austro-Hungarian Navy, pp. 132-33; Dragan R. Zivojinovic, "The Emergence of American Policy in the Adriatic: December 1917-April 1919," East European Quarterly 1 (Sept. 1967):176-81.

44. NARG 38, Naval Attaché Reports. "The Sinking of the Zent Istvan, June 9-10, 1918"; MI, 7:254, 291-92, 298, 334-38, 510-12, 545-73, 8:113;14; Hazlett, "Davids of the Sea," pp. 1037-38.

45. Sims to Benson, 21 Aug., 17 Sept., 11 Oct. 1918, Sims Papers; Manfroni, I Nostri alleati navale, pp. 262-68; MI, 8:11-112, 332-34; Ray Millholland, The Splinter Fleet on the Otranto Barrage. New York: Bobbs-Merrill, 1936, pp. 220-40 and Appendix B., pp. 302-7; Roma. Ufficio Storico della R. Marina, Preparazione dei mezzi e loro impiego, 12 vols. Vol. 5. Sbarramento del Canale d'Otranto, and Vol. 7. Bombardamento di Durazzo (nel 1918); Thomazi, La Guerre navale dans l'Adriatique, pp. 196-98.

46. Bagnasco, I MAS e le Motosiluranti, p. 619; Lega Navale Italiana, La Marina Italiana nella guerra mondiale, pp. 156-61; MI, 7:434-50; Sokol, Austro-Hungarian Navy, p. 124; Thomazi, La Guerre navale dans l'Adriatique, pp. 201-2.

47. NARG, Naval Attaché Reports, 24-25 Oct., 7 Nov. 1918; MI, 8:585-95; Halpern, Naval War in the Mediterranean, pp. 498-578.

48. MI, 8:509-19; Commandante Guido Po, Il Grande Ammiraglio Paolo Thaon di Revel. Torino: S. Lattes & C. Editori, 1936, pp. 194-96; Usborne, Smoke on the Horizon, pp. 306-18; Hazlett, "Davids of the Sea," pp. 1040-46; "Medaglia d'oro Raffale Paolucci (1 Giugno 1892-4 Settembre 1958)," Rivista Marittima 91 (Sept. 1959):5-16.

49. L'Italia e la fine della Guerra Mondiale: Villa Giusti. Roma: Stato Maggiore dell'Esercito. Ufficio Storico, 1925; MI, 8:619-35; Train in

NARG 38, Naval Attaché Reports, 6 Nov. 1918.

50. Manfroni, I Nostri alleati navale, pp. 276-79;
MI, 8:641-55; Alfacanis, "Umberto Cagni," Rivista Marittima 96 (Feb. 1963):15-28. A list
of the territory occupied by Italy at or soon
after the time of the armistice is available in
Po, Di Revel, Appendix 4, pp. 292-93.

CHAPTER 9

1. At least this was the conclusion in "Lessons of
the War: A French Admiral's Views." Trans. by
LT C.F. Jepson, RUSIJ 65 (Oct. 1920):593.

2. Paul M. Kennedy, The Rise and Fall of British
Naval Mastery. London: Allan Lane, 1976, p.
245; Arthur J. Marder, From the Dreadnought to
Scapa Flow: The Royal Navy in the Fisher Era,
1904-1919, 5 vols. New York: Oxford University
Press, 1961-1966, 5:288-89; Alfred von Tirpitz,
My Memoirs, 2 vols. New York: Dodd, Mead, 1919,
2:366; William Seaver Woods, Colossal Blunders
of the War. New York: Macmillan, 1931.

3. Arthur J. Marder, "The Influence of History on
Sea Power: The Royal Navy and the Lessons of
1914-1918," Pacific Historical Review 41 (Nov.
1972):413-43.

4. Paolo E. Coletta, "Josephus Daniels." In Paolo
E. Coletta, Robert G. Albion, and K. Jack Bauer,
eds. American Secretaries of the Navy, 2 vols.
Annapolis, Md.: Naval Institute Press, 1980,
2:565-72; Tracy B. Kittredge, Naval Lessons of
the Great War. . . . Garden City, N.Y.: Doubleday, Page, 1921, which closely follows the two
million words of testimony transcribed in U.S.
Congress, Senate Naval Affairs Committee, Hearings before the Subcommittee of the Committee
on Naval Affairs, 2 vols. Washington: GPO,
1920; and Dean C. Allard, "Admiral William S.
Sims and U. S. Naval Policy in World War I,"
American Neptune 35 (Apr. 1975):97-110.

SELECTED SOURCES

Helpful in understanding Austria's diplomatic and domestic affairs are C.J. Lowe, From Sadowa to Sarajevo: The Foreign Policy of Austria-Hungary 1866-1914. Boston: Routledge & Kegan Paul, 1972; Arthur J. May, The Passing of the Habsburg Monarchy 1914-1918, 2 vols. Philadelphia: University of Pennsylvania Press, 1946, and The Habsburg Monarchy, 1867-1914. Cambridge, Mass.: Harvard University Press, 1951; Austria-Hungary. The Secret Treaties of Austria-Hungary, 2 vols. Ed. A.F. Pribam. Cambridge, Mass.: Harvard University Press, 1920-1921; Edward von Glaise-Horstenau, The Collapse of the Austro-Hungarian Empire. Trans. Ian F.D. Morrow. London: J.M. Dent, 1930. For military affairs there are Gunther Rothenberg, The Army of Francis Joseph. West Lafayette, Ind.: Purdue University Press, 1976; Anthony E. Sokol, The Imperial and Royal Austro-Hungarian Navy. Annapolis, Md.: U.S. Naval Institute, 1968; "Austria-Hungary's Naval Building Projects, 1914-1918. Part I. Cruisers," Warships International 15, No. 3, 1978, pp. 184-99, and R. F. de Heere Scheltema. Ed. by C.W. Wright, "Austro-Hungarian Battleships," Warships International 10, No. 1, 1973, pp. 11-97. Nicholas Horthy, Memoirs. New York: Roger Speller & Sons, 1957, tells of his activities while serving in and then commanding the Austrian fleet.

Personal histories of important French personages include MGEN Sir George Aston, The Biography of the Late Marshal Foch. New York: Macmillan, 1929; Vice amiral Dartige du Fournet, Souvenirs de guerre d'un amiral. Paris; Plon, 1920; Ferdinand Foch, The Memoirs of Marshal Foch. Trans. by Col. T. Bentley Mott. Garden City, N.Y.: Doubleday, Doran, 1931; Raymond Poincare, Memoirs. New York: Doubleday, Doran, 1931; and Raymond Recouly, Joffre. New York: D. Appleton, 1931.

Among general works on the French Navy, see Paul Chack and Jean-Jacques Antier, Histoire Maritime de la premier guerre mondiale, 3 vols. Paris: Editions France-Empire, 1969; J. Labayle Couhat, French Warships of World War I. London: Ian Allen, 1974;

159

Louis Guichard, The Naval Blockade 1914-1918. Trans. and ed. by Christopher Turner. London: Philip Allen, 1930; com.t Adolphe Laurens, Le Commandement naval en Mediterranee 1914-1918. Paris: Payot, 1931, and Precis d'Histoire de la guerre navale 1914-1918. Paris: Payot, 1929; Louis Nicolas, Histoire de la Marine Francaise. Paris: Presses Universitaires de France, 1949; Albert Pingaud, Histoire diplomatique de la France pendant la grand guerre, 3 vols. Paris: Alsatia, 1935-1945; Jean Randier, La Royale: L'Eperon et la Cuirasse. Brest: Editions de la Cite, 1972; and CAPT Auguste A. Thomazi, French Navy, La Guerre navale dans l'Adriatique. Paris: Payot, 1925. An interesting evaluation is that by Major T.A. Gibson, "Foch: The First Supreme Commander," Military Affairs 42 (Apr. 1978):61-67. Two excellent doctoral dissertations are: Andre Kaspi, "Le Temps des Americains: Le concours Americaines a la France en 1914-1918." Université de Paris, 1976, and Yves-Henri Nouilhat, "France et États-Unis, aout 1914-avril 1917." Paris; Publications de la Sorbonne, 1979.

Although the first volumes of the official German history of the naval war appeared in 1922, the last did not see light until the late 1960s, and not all the volumes translated into English are available in the United States. By courtesy of J. David Brown, of the Naval History Library, London, England, I was able to read in English translation the following volumes, all published by Berlin: E.S. Mittler and Son: Otto Groos, Der Krieg in der Nordsee (The War in the North Sea), 5 vols., and Walter Gladisch, The War in the North Sea, vols. 6 and 7; Arno Spindler, Der Handelskrieg mit U-Booten (The Commerce War in Submarines), 5 vols; and Paul Koeppen, The Surface Forces and Their Techniques, vol. 7. An extremely useful collection of documents is that edited by Ralph H. Lutz, Causes of the German Collapse in 1918. . . , 2 vols. Hamden, Conn.: Shoe String Press, 1934. A mammoth collection is that by Keith Bird, German Naval History: A Guide to the Literature. New York: Garland, 1985.

Seven personal histories proved most vital in understanding German military and naval actions are: GEN [Erich] von Falkenhayn, The German General Staff and Its Decisions, 1914-1916. New York: Dodd, Mead, 1920; CDR Georg von Hase (First Gunnery Officer of the Derfflinger), Kiel and Jutland. Trans. Arthur Chambers and F.A. Holt. London: Skeffington & Sons, 1921; Marshal Paul von Hindenburg, Out of My Life.

London: Cassell, 1920; Erich von Ludendorff, Luden-dorff's Own Story, 2 vols. New York: Harper, 1919; ADM Scheer, Germany's High Sea Fleet in the World War. New York: Peter Smith, 1934; Alfred von Tirpitz, My Memoirs, 2 vols. New York: Dodd, Mead, 1919; and Hugo von Waldeyer-Hartz, Admiral von Hipper. Trans. D. Appleby Holt. London: Rich & Cowan, 1933. The Kaiser's memoirs are barely useful, and to date there is no truly satisfactory biography of him.

Helpful general works on the German Navy of World War I are: Karl E. Birnbaum, Peace Moves and U-boat Warfare: A Study of Imperial Germany's Policy toward the United States, April 18, 1916-January 9, 1917. Stockholm: Almquist & Wiksell, 1958; Carl-Axel Gemzell, Organization, Conflict, and Innovation: A Study of German Naval Strategic Planning. Stockholm: Usselte Studium, 1973; Holger H. Herwig, "Luxury Fleet": The Imperial German Navy, 1888-1918. London: George Allen & Unwin, 1980, and Politics of Frustra-tion: The United States in German Naval Planning, 1889-1941. Boston: Little, Brown, 1976; Paul Schma-lenbach, German Raiders: A History of Auxiliary Cruisers of the German Navy, 1895-1942. Annapolis, Md.: Naval Institute Press, 1979; Charles F. Sidman, The German Collapse in 1918. Lawrence, Kans.: Coro-nado Press, 1973; Jonathan Steinberg, Yesterday's Deterrent: Tirpitz and the Birth of the German Bat-tle Fleet. New York: Macmillan, 1965. For ship characteristics, see John Charles Taylor, German Warships of World War I. Garden City, N.Y.: Double-day, 1970, and Jans Jurgen Hansen, The Ships of the German Fleets, 1848-1945, 2d ed., Annapolis, Md: Naval Institute Press, 1988.

Helpful articles are: Albert Gayer, "Summary of German Submarine Operations in the Various Theaters of War from 1914 to 1918," USNIP 52 (Apr. 1926):621-59; Philip K. Lundeberg, "Underseas War-fare and Allied Strategy in World War I. Part I: to 1916," The Smithsonian Journal of History 1 (Autumn 1966):1-30. and Part II, ibid., (Winter 1966):47-72, and "The German Naval Critique of the U-Boat Campaign, 1915-1918," Military Affairs, 27 (Fall 1963):109-13.; and Arno Spindler, "The Value of the Submarine Warfare," USNIP 52 (May 1926):835-54.

Selected British official documents include: Great Britain. Admiralty. Battle of Jutland. London: HMSO, 1924; Battle of Jutland: Maps. London: HMSO,

1920; <u>Battle of Jutland: Official Despatches</u>. London: HMSO, 1916; Office of the Chief of Staff of the Royal Navy (Historical Section), <u>Authentic History of the Italian-Austro-Hungarian Naval War, 1915-1918</u>. Copy by Washington: Navy Department, ONI, 1920; Archibald C. Bell, <u>A History of the Blockade of Germany and of the Countries Associated with Her in the Great War, 1914-1918</u>. London: HMSO, 1936, 1961; Julian S. Corbett and Henry Newbolt, <u>History of the Great War, Based on Official Documents: Naval Operations</u>, 5 vols. London: Longmans, Green, 1920-1931; C. Ernest Fayle, <u>Seaborne Trade: History of the Great War Based on Official Documents</u>, 3 vols. New York: Longmans, Green, 1923; Archibald Hurd, <u>The Merchant Navy: History of the Great War Based on Official Documents</u>, 3 vols. London: John Murray, 1921-1929; and Sir Walter Raleigh and Henry A. Jones, <u>The War in the Air: Official History of the War, Based on Official Documents</u>, 6 vols. Oxford: Clarendon Press, 1922-1934.

Extremely useful are <u>Brassey's Naval Annual</u>, various publishers, 1886- ; <u>Naval Review</u>, vols. 1-14, 1913-1926; and <u>The Times Documentary History of the War</u>, 11 vols. London: <u>The Times</u>, 1917-1920; <u>British Naval and Military Record and Royal Dockyards Gazette</u>. London and Plymouth: <u>The Western Morning News</u>, 1833-1934; and <u>Mariner's Mirror</u>, The Society for Nautical Research, vol. 1- , 1910- .

Primary personal histories include: A. Altham, CAPT, RN, <u>Jellicoe</u>. London: Blackie, 1938; ADM Sir Reginald H. Bacon, <u>The Life of Lord Fisher of Kilverstone</u>, 2 vols. Garden City, N.Y.: Doubleday, 1929, and <u>The Life of John Rushworth, Earl Jellicoe</u>. London: Cassell, 1936; ADM Sir Lewis Bayly, <u>Pull Together: The Memoirs of Admiral Sir Lewis Bayly</u>. London: George G. Harrap, 1939; Charles Beatty, <u>Our Admiral: A Biography of Admiral of the Fleet Earl Beatty</u>. London: W.H. Allen, 1980; Violet Bonham-Carter, <u>Winston Churchill: An Intimate Portrait</u>. New York: Harcourt, Brace, 1965; Andrew Boyle, <u>Trenchard</u>. London: Collins, 1962; RADM William Scott Chalmers, <u>The</u> [sanitized] <u>Life and Letters of David Beatty, Admiral of the Fleet</u>. London: Hodder and Stoughton, 1931; Robert H. Dawson, <u>Winston Churchill at the Admiralty</u>. Toronto: University of Toronto Press, 1949 [an unrelieved panegyric] ; David Lloyd George, <u>War Memoirs of David Lloyd George</u>, 6 vols. Boston: Little, Brown, 1933-1937; Martin Gilbert, <u>Winston Churchill</u>, 5 vols. Boston: Houghton Mifflin,

1966-1987; Lord Hankey, The Supreme Command, 2 vols.
London: George Allen and Unwin, 1961; ADM Mark E.F.
Kerr, Land, Sea, and Air: Reminiscences of Mark Kerr.
New York: Longmans, Green, 1927, and Prince Louis of
Battenberg: Admiral of the Fleet. London: Longmans,
Green, 1934; Roger Keyes, The Naval Memoirs of Ad-
miral of the Fleet Roger Keyes, 2 vols. New York:
E.P. Dutton, 1934-1935; A. Temple Patterson, Jelli-
coe: A Biography. London: Macmillan, 1969, and
Tyrwhitt of the Harwich Force: The Life of Admiral
of the Fleet Reginald Tyrwhitt. London: Macdonald,
1973; Sir James Rennel Rodd, Social and Diplomatic
Memories (Third Series), 1902-1919. London: Edward
Arnold, 1925; Stephen W. Roskill, Admiral of the
Fleet Earl Beatty. The Last Naval Hero: An Intimate
Biography [warts and all]. New York: Atheneum, 1984;
Murray F. Sueter, Airman or Noahs: Fair Play for our
Airmen. . . . London: Sir Isaac Pitman and Sons,
1928; Viscount Grey of Fallodon, Twenty-five Years,
1892-1916, 2 vols. New York: Frederick A. Stokes
Co., 1925; and Lady Wester Wemyss, The Life and
Letters of Lord Wester Wemyss. London: Eyre and
Spottiswoode, 1935.

Among the plethora of general works, see Sir
Reginald Bacon, The Concise Story of the Dover Pa-
trol. London: Hutchinson, 1932, and The Jutland
Scandal, 4th ed. London: Hutchinson, n.d.; John M.
Bruce, British Aeroplanes, 1914-1918. London: Putnam,
1957; A.F.B. Carpenter, The Blocking of Zeebrugge.
London: Jenkins, 1962; Kathleen Burk, Britain, Amer-
ica and the Sinews of War, 1914-1915. Boston: George
Allen & Unwin, 1985; Winston Churchill, The World
Crisis, 4 vols. in 1. New York: Charles Scribner's
Sons, 1931; C.R.M.P. Cruttwell, A History of the
Great War 1914-1918, 2d ed. Oxford: Clarendon Press,
1936; K.G.B. Dewar, The Navy from Within. London:
Victor Gollancz, 1939; David French, British Economic
and Strategic Planning 1905-1914. Winchester, Mass.:
Allen & Unwin, 1982; Leslie Gardiner, The British
Admiralty. Edinburgh and London: William Blackwood &
Sons, 1968; Richard H. Gibson and Maurice Prender-
gast, The German Submarine War 1914-1918. New York:
Richard R. Smith, 1931; Robert M. Grant, U-boats
Destroyed: The Effect of Anti-Submarine Warfare
1914-1918. London: Putnam, 1974; Trumbull Higgins,
Winston Churchill and the Dardanelles: A Dialogue
in Ends and Means. New York: Macmillan, 1964; Admiral
of the Fleet Jellicoe, The Submarine Peril: The Ad-
miralty Policy in 1917. London: Cassell, 1934, The
Crisis of the Naval War. London: Cassell, 1920, and

The Grand Fleet 1914-1916; Its Creation, Development
and Work. New York: George H. Doran, 1919; Paul M.
Kennedy, The Rise and Fall of British Naval Mastery.
London: Allan Lane, 1987; Esmond W.W.B. Lunby, ed.
Policy and Operations in the Mediterranean 1912-1915.
Navy Records Society, 115. London: William Clowes,
1970; Arthur J. Marder, From the Dardanelles to
Oran: Studies in the Royal Navy in War and Peace,
1915-1940. New York: Oxford University Press, 1974,
From the Dreadnought to Scapa Flow: The Royal Navy
in the Fisher Era, 1904-1919, 5 vols. New York:
Oxford University Press, 1961-1966, and Fear God and
Dread Nought: The Correspondence of Admiral of the
Fleet Lord Fisher of Kilverstone, 2 vols. Cambridge,
Mass.: Harvard University Press, 1925; Sir Frederick
Maurice, Lessons of Allied Cooperation: Naval, Mili-
tary, and Air, 1914-1918. New York: Oxford University
Press, 1942; Keith Nelson, Strategy and Supply: The
Anglo-Russian Alliance 1914-1917. London: Allen &
Unwin, 1984; Randolph Pears, British Battleships
1892-1957: Great Days of the Fleets. London: Putnam,
1957; James R. Salter, Allied Shipping Control: An
Experiment in International Administration, 3 vols.
Oxford: Clarendon Press, 1921; VADM Cecil Vivian Usborne, Smoke on the Horizon: Mediterranean Fighting
1914-1918. London: Hodder and Stoughton, 1933; H.W.
Wilson, Battleships in Action, 2 vols. Boston: Little, Brown, 1926; and Sir Llewellen Woodward, Great
Britain and the War of 1914-1918. London: Methuen,
1967. Although John Campbell, Jutland: An Analysis
of the Fighting. Annapolis, Md.: Naval Institute
Press, 1986, avoids strategic considerations, he
accounts for the damage done by the guns of all ships
upon the enemy.

Several articles pertinent to the naval aspects
of the war are: Nicholas D'Ombrain, "Churchill at the
Admiralty," RUSIJ 115 (Mar. 19780):38-41; Paul Hag-
gie, "Royal Navy and War Planning in the Fisher Era,"
Journal of Contemporary History 7 (Apr. 1972):161-70;
I.L.M. McGeoch, CAPT, RN, "Sea Power and the Darda-
nelles," RUSIJ 101 (Nov. 1956):580-86; T.H. Thomas,
"British War Policy and the Western Front," Foreign
Affairs 1 (June 15, 1922):153-62; David Woodward,
"The High Seas Fleet: 1917-1918," RUSIJ 113 (Aug.
1968):244-50; and Esmond Wright, "The Foreign Policy
of Woodrow Wilson: a Reassessment. Part I.," History
Today 10 (Mar. 1960):149-57, and Part II, ibid., 10
(Apr. 1960):223-31.

Among the many titles published by the Italian

Defense Ministry or Department of the Army, interest centers upon: Roma: Ministero della Difesa. State Maggiore dell'Esercito. Ufficio Storico. L'Esercito italiano nella grande Guerra (1915-1918), 7 vols. The basic narrative of the Italian Navy's history office is La Marina italiana nella grande Guerra, 8 vols. Firenze: Vallecchi Editore, 1935-1942. The same office has also published two valuable series. As translated into English, their titles are Preparation of Means and Their Employment, 12 vols., and Employment of Naval Forces: Operations, 16 vols. A wartime diary and short comments on the principle naval events of the war are available in Lega Navale Italiana, La Marina Italiana nella Guerra Mondiale.

While some excellent articles are found in Rivista Storica Italiana, more specialized studies are found in Rivista Marittima, which has been published in Rome by the Ministero della Marina since 1867. I have read its monthly issues from 1913 to date. Two articles in English are also pertinent: "Action of May 15th, 1917, in the Adriatic, and the Torpedoing of the Dartmouth, " Naval Review 7 (1919):379-84, and Nicholas U.N. Slankovic, Capt. RYSN, "The War in the Adriatic 1914-1918," Naval Review 11 (1923):459-75.

Pertinent general works for Italy include: A. Balliano and G. Soavi, L'Italia sul mare nella grande guerra. Torino: G. Einaudi, 1934; Iunio V. Borghese, Sea Devils. Trans. James Clough from the original, Decima Flottiglia mas. London: Melrose, 1955; Mario Caracciolo, L'Italia ed i suoi alleati nella grande guerra. Milano: A. Mondadori, 1932; Aldo Fraccaroli, Italian Warships of World War I. London: Ian Allan, 1968; Angiolo Ginocchetti, La Guerra sul mare. Roma: A. Mondadori, 1930; Archibald Hurd, Italian Sea Power and the Great War. London: Constable, 1918; C.J. Lowe and F. Marzari, Italian Foreign Policy 1870-1940. Boston: Routledge & Kegan Paul, 1975; Camillo Manfroni, I Nostri alleati navale: Ricordi della guerra Adriatica, 1915-1918. Milano: A. Mondadori, 1927, and Storia della marina italiana durante la guerra mondiale, 1914-1918. Bologna: N. Zanichelli, 1923; Thomas Nelson Page, Italy and the World War. London: Chapman and Hall, 1921; Guido Po, La Guerra marittima dell'italia. Milano: Corbaccio, 1934, and Il Grande ammiraglio Paolo Thaon di Revel. Torino: S. Lattes & C., Editori, 1936; Generale Sq. A. Felice Porro, La Guerra nel aria 1915-1918. Milano: Edizione Mates, 1935; Edward A. Powell, Italy at War and the Allies in the West. New York: Charles Scribner's Sons, 1917; Antonio Salandra, Italy and the Great War: From Neutrality to Intervention. Trans. by Zoe Kendrick Pyne. London: Edward Arnold, 1932; Fabbi Slafhek, Con gli inglesi in Adriatico. Roma: Ardita, 1934; A. Torre and others, La Politica estera italiana dal 1914 al 1943. Torino: ERI, 1963; Mario Toscano, Alto Adige-South Tyrol: Italy's Frontier with the German World. Ed. George A. Carbone. Baltimore: Johns Hopkins Press, 1976; Luigi Villari, The War on the Italian Front. London: Cobden Sanderson, 1932; and Dragan R. Zivojinojic, America, Italy, and the Birth of Yugoslavia (1917-1919). Boulder: East European Quarterly. Distributed by New York: Columbia University Press, 1972. Extremely thorough is Paul G. Halpern, The Naval War in the Mediterranean 1914-1918. Annapolis, Md.: Naval Institute Press, 1987.

Most rewarding of the papers in the Manuscript Division of the Library of Congress are those of William S. Benson, William J. Bryan, Bradley Allen Fiske, Washington Irving Chambers, Josephus Daniels, Albert Gleaves, Dudley W. Knox, Robert Lansing, William V. Pratt, Joseph Strauss, Joseph K. Taussig, Woodrow Wilson, and Harry L. Yarnell. The papers, including the diary, of Edward M. House, were used at the Sterling Memorial Library, Yale University.

Other doctoral dissertations found useful included: Edward H. Brooks, "The National Defense Policy of the Wilson Administration, 1913-1917." Stanford University; CDR Joseph Costello, USN, "Planning for War: A History of the General Board of the Navy, 1900-1914." Fletcher School of Law and Diplomacy, 1968; Jeremiah N. Fusco, "The Diplomatic Relations between the United Sates and Austria, 1913-1917." George Washington University, 1969; Charles H. Hunter, "Anglo-American Relations during the Period of American Belligerency, 1917-1918." Stanford University, 1935; Mary Klachko, "Anglo-American Naval Competition, 1918-1922." Columbia University, 1962; and Warner R. Schilling, "Admirals and Foreign Policy, 1913-1919." Yale University, 1957.

The official story of American naval activity is told in the Annual Report of the Secretary of the Navy. Extremely useful, in the National Archives, are NARG 24, Records of Naval Officers and Ships' Logs; NARG 38, Records of the Office of Chief of Naval Operations, including Naval Attaché Reports;

NARG 45, Naval Records Collection of the Office of Naval Records and Library; NARG 80, General Correspondence of the Secretary of the Navy; and NARG 313, Records of Naval Operating Forces.

Most important among the many monographs published from the holdings in NARG 45 are: German Submarine Activities on the Atlantic Coast of the United States and Canada. Washington: 1920, and The United States Naval Railway Batteries in France. Washington, 1922. Also under official imprint are Ralph Earle, ed. Naval Ordnance Activities: World War 1917-1918. Washington: GPO, 1920; U.S. Naval Aviation, 1910-1960. Washington: GPO, 1960; U.S. Navy Department. ONI. Historical Section. Pub. No. 7. American Naval Planning Section in London. Washington: GPO, 1923; and U.S. AEF. Final Report of General John J. Pershing Commander-in-Chief American Expeditionary Forces. Washington: GPO, 1919.

In addition to the Records of the General Board of the Navy for the years 1913-1912, I have used its minutes, published as Proceedings. These are in Washington: Naval Historical Center, Operational Archives Branch.

Detailed information on American naval affairs has been garnered from the annual hearings on the estimates submitted by the secretary of the Navy for the years 1914-1919. Admiral Sims's postwar charges of incompetence in Washington and the rebuttals to them are available in Naval Investigation: Hearings Before the Subcommittee of the Committee on Naval Affairs, U.S. Senate, 66th Cong., 2d Sess., 2 vols. Washington: GPO, 1921.

Diplomatic events for the years 1913-1919 were followed in several of the decimal files of the U.S. Department of State and in its Papers Relating to the Foreign Relations of the United States, 1861- .

Good coverage of maritime and naval affairs is found in such American newspapers as the Baltimore Sun, New York American, New York Herald, New York Journal, New York Times, New York World, and Washington Post. The American Review of Reviews, Army and Navy Journal, Army and Navy Register, and Literary Digest contain excellent summaries and editorial comments. Many articles critical of the Navy in addition to those on professional matters grace the pages of the U.S. Naval Institute Proceedings, while

Current History provides in-depth coverage of issues. Although accounts of naval and foreign affairs are carried in such literary journals as the Atlantic Monthly, Forum, Harper's, and North American Review (which was uproariously anti-Daniels), specialized studies on naval matters appear in the American Neptune, Military Affairs, Scientific American, and Warships International. Historical articles dealing with events of the neutrality and war years are also found in American Historical Review, Historian, The Mississippi Valley Historical Review (later Journal of American History), and Pacific Historical Review.

An extremely selective list of important signed articles in the magazines noted above and in others follows. Dean C. Allard, "Anglo-American Naval Differences during World War I, " Military Affairs 44 (Apr. 1980):75-81, and "Admiral William S. Sims and United States Naval Policy in World War I," American Neptune 35 (Apr. 1975):95-110; Tasker H. Bliss, "The Evolution of the United Command," Foreign Affairs 1 (Dec. 15, 1922):1-30; Paolo E. Coletta, "The United States and Italy in the Allied Naval Council of World War I." In Atti del 1 Congresso Internazionale di Storia Americana. . . . Genova, 26-29 maggio, 1976. Genova: Tilgher, 1978, pp. 91-102, and "The United States Navy in the Adriatic in World War I." In Timothy J. Runyan, ed. Ships, Seafaring and Society: Essays in Maritime History. Detroit: Wayne State University, 1987, pp. 339-54; Bradley A. Fiske, "Torpedo Plane and Bomber," USNIP 48 (Sept. 1922):1474-78; Julius A. Furer, "The 110-Foot Submarine Chasers and Eagle Boats," USNIP 45 (May 1919):743-52' E.E. Hazlett, "Davids of the Sea," USNIP 54 (Dec. 11928):1035-46; Alice M. Morrissey, "The United States and the Rights of Neutrals, 1917-1918," American Journal of International Law 31 (Jan. 1937):17-30; Charles Seymour, "American Neutrality: The Experience of 1914-1917," Foreign Affairs 14 (Oct. 1935):26-36; Joseph K. Taussig, "Destroyer Experiences during the Great War," USNIP 48 (Dec. 1922):2015-40 and 49 (Jan.-Mar. 1923):36-69; and Norman Van der Meer, "Mining Operations in the War," USNIP 45 (Nov. 1919):1857-65.

The most important American personal histories are: Paolo E. Coletta, William Jennings Bryan: Progressive Politician and Moral Statesman, 1909-1915. Lincoln: University of Nebraska Press, 1969, and Admiral Bradley A. Fiske and the American Navy. Lawrence: Regents Press of Kansas, 1979; Josephus

Daniels, The Wilson Era: Years of War, 1917-1923. Chapel Hill: University of North Carolina Press, 1946; E. David Cronon, ed. The Cabinet Diaries of Josephus Daniels, 1913-1921. Lincoln: University of Nebraska Press, 1963; Frank B. Freidel, Franklin D. Roosevelt: The Apprenticeship. Boston: Little, Brown, Frank E. Vandiver, Black Jack: The Life and Times of John J. Pershing, 2 vols. College Station and London: Texas A&M Press, 1977; Burton J. Hendrick, The Life and Letters of Walter H. Page, 3 vols. Garden City, N.Y.: Doubleday, Page, 1924-1926; and Mary Klachko with David F. Trask, Admiral William Shepherd Benson: First Chief of Naval Operations. Annapolis, Md.: Naval Institute Press, 1987. Edward N. Hurley has provided an autobiographical account of his leadership of the U.S. Shipping Board in The Bridge to France. Philadelphia: J.B. Lippincott, 1927. See also Robert Lansing, War Memoirs of Robert Lansing, Secretary of State. New York: Bobbs-Merrill, 1935. Two excellent accounts are Elting E. Morison, Admiral Sims and the Modern American Navy. Boston: Houghton Mifflin 1942, and MGEN John A. Lejeune, USMC, Reminiscences of a Marine. Philadelphia: Dorrance, 1930.

Of the many biographies of Woodrow Wilson, the best is the one Arthur S. Link, as yet not completed: Wilson, 5 vols. Princeton, N.J.: Princeton University Press, 1947- . Capably edited is Charles Seymour, The Intimate Papers of Colonel House, 4 vols. Boston: Houghton Mifflin, 1926-1928. Very judiciously sanitized of criticism of the Wilson administration is RADM William Sowden Sims, U.S. Navy, in collaboration with Burton J. Hendrick, The Victory at Sea. Garden City, N.Y.: Doubleday, Page, 1920. With great skill, Gerald E. Wheeler has recounted the efforts of the Assistant Chief of Naval Operations during the war years in Admiral William Veazie Pratt, U.S. Navy: A Sailor's Life. Washington: Naval History Division, 1974.

Among the best general works on the U.S. Navy are: K. Jack Bauer, Ships of the Navy, 1775-1969: Combat Vessels. Troy, N.Y.: Rensselaer Polytechnic Institute, 1970; U.S. Department of the Navy. Naval History Division, Dictionary of American Naval Fighting Ships, 8 vols., 1959-1981; Lewis P. Clephane, comp. History of the Naval Overseas Transportation Service in World War I. Washington: Naval History Division, 1969; Ray Millholland, The Splinter Fleet on the Otranto Barrage. New York: Bobbs-Merrill, 1936; Alexander W. Moffatt, Maverick Navy. Middletown, Conn.: Weslyan University Press, 1976; William C. Mattox, Building the Emergency Fleet. 1920; reprinted New York: Library Editions, 1970.

On air power I have relied upon Patrick Abbot, Airship. New York: Charles Scribner's Sons, 1973; Roger A. Caras, The Story of U.S. Naval Aviation: Wings of Gold. Philadelphia: J.B. Lippincott, 1965; Archibald D. Turnbull and Clifford L. Lord, History of United States Naval Aviation. New Haven: Yale University Press, 1949; and Adrian O. Van Wyen, Naval Aviation in World War I. Washington: Chief of Naval Operations, 1969.

Selected titles that deal with diplomacy that affected military and naval affairs during the Great War include: Thomas A. Bailey, The Policy of the United States toward the Neutrals, 1917-1918. Baltimore: Johns Hopkins Press, 1942; James W. Garner, International Law and the World War, 2 vols. New York: Longmans, Green, 1920; George B. Leon, Greece and the Great Powers, 1914-1917. Salonika: Institute for Balkan Studies, 1974; Arthur S. Link, Woodrow Wilson: Revolution, War, and Peace. Arlington Heights, Ill.: AHM Press, 1979; Jeffrey J. Safford, Wilsonian Maritime Diplomacy, 1912-1921. New Brunswick, N.J.: Rutgers University Press, 1978; Charles Seymour, American Diplomacy during the World War. Baltimore: Johns Hopkins Press, 1934; David F. Trask, Captains & Cabinets: Anglo-American Naval Relations 1917-1918. Columbia: University of Missouri Press, 1972, and The United States in the Supreme War Council: American War Aims and Inter-Allied Strategy, 1917-1918. Middletown, Conn.: Weslyan University Press, 1961; and Z.A.B. Zeman, The Gentleman Negotiators: A Diplomatic History of World War I. New York: Macmillan, 1971.

The following titles deal variously with diplomatic, industrial, economic, military, Marine Corps, or naval matters: Wilbur V. Van Auken, Notes on a Half Century of U.S. Naval Ordnance, 1880-1931. Washington: George Banta, 1939: Benedict Crowell and Robert F. Wilson, The Road to France: The Transportation of Troops and Military Supplies, 1917-1918, 2 vols. New Haven: Yale University Press; Grosvenor Clarkson, Industrial America in the World War: The Strategy Behind the Lines. Boston: Houghton Mifflin, 1923; Thomas G. Frothingham, The Naval History of the World War, 3 vols. Cambridge, Mass.: Harvard

University Press, 1914-1926; Charles Gilbert, <u>Amer-ican Financing of World War I</u>. Westport, Conn.: Greenwood Press, 1970; Albert Gleaves, <u>History of the Transport Service: Experiences of U.S. Transports and Cruisers in the World War</u>. New York: George H. Doran, 1921; Gregory Hartmann, <u>Weapons that Wait</u> [mines]. Annapolis, Md.: Naval Institute Press, 1979; Reginald W. Kauffman, <u>Our Navy at Work: The Yankee Navy in French Waters</u>. Indianapolis: Bobbs-Merrill, 1918; William G. Lyddon, <u>British War Mis-sions to the Untied States 1914-1918</u>. New York: Oxford University Press, 1938; Allan R. Millett, <u>Semper Fidelis: The History of the United States Marine Corps</u>. New York: Macmillan, 1980; Lloyd N. Scott, <u>Naval Consulting Board of the United States</u>. Washington: GPO, 1920; Charles Seymour, <u>American Neutrality, 1914-1917</u>. New Haven: Yale University Press, 1935.

The following have a bearing upon Allied-Turkish relations during the war: Ahmed Emin, <u>Turkey in the World War</u>. New Haven: Yale University Press, 1930; Liman von Sanders, <u>Five Years in Turkey</u>. Annapolis, Md.: U.S.Naval Institute, 1927; Ulrich Trumpener, "Liman von Sanders and the German-Ottoman Alliance," <u>Journal of Contemporary History</u> 1 (Oct. 1966):179-82. Pertinent also is Rene Greger, <u>The Russian Fleet, 1914-1917</u>. Trans. from the German by Jill Gearing. London: Ian Allen, 1972.

Adm., 60, 61, 62, 64, 75-76

Milne, Sir Berkeley, Br. Adm., and the "escape" of the Goeben and Breslau, 9-10

Monro, Sir Charles, Br. Gen., 22

Naval armistice terms for Austria, 119

Naval armistice terms for Germany, 82-85

Naval Overseas Transportation Service, 67, 70-1, 73

Nivelle, Robert, Fr. Gen., 46

North Sea Mine Barrage, 71-72

Ostfriesland, Ger. battleship, 42

Otranto Strait Mine Barrage, 93, 98, 107, 118

Page, Walter Hines, 56

Pershing, John J., U.S. Gen., 65, 78-79

Pohl, Hugo von, Ger. Adm., 28, 34

Pratt, William Veazie, USN, 60

Q Ships, 26

Rizzo, Luigi, It. Navy, 117, 118

Roosevelt, Franklin D., 53, 74

Sarrail, Maurice, Fr. Gen., 22, 105

Scheer, Reinhard, Ger. Adm.: 17, 34, 36, 44, 47; and the Battle of Jutland, 37-44; and his failed suicide attack, 81-82, 85

Sea power: British debate proper use of, 18-19,

21-22; and its contributions to Allied victory, 123-25

Seidlitz, Ger. battle cruiser, 18

Serbia: 2, 22; and the rescue of her army, 105-6

Sims, William S., U.S. Adm., 51, 54-55, 56, 60, 61, 62, 64, 68, 75, 76, 78, 126-27

Sueter, Murray F., Br. Adm., 46, 111

Supreme War Council, 23, 64

Sussex, Fr. ferry, 36

Tirpitz, Alfred von, Ger. Grand Adm.: 25, 26, 33, 35; and his assumptions about war, 5-6

Treaty of: London, May 1915, 21; and of Brest Litovsk, 3 Mar. 1918, 79

Tyrwhitt, Sir Reginald, Br. Adm., 17

U-boats: in the First Battle of the Atlantic, 25-36, 44-48, 53-65, 77, 79-80, 81-82; and in the Mediterranean, 95, 98, 112-13, 117

Weddigen, Otto, Ger. Navy, 13, 16

Wemyss, Sir Rosslyn Wester, Br. Adm., 57, 59, 73, 116

Wilhelm, Ger. Kaiser and Emperor, 1, 13, 18, 35, 36, 118 36, 116

Wilson, Sir Arthur, Br. Adm., 4

Wilson, President Woodrow: 28, 35, 61, 62, 78; and his mediation attempt, Dec. 1915, 47;